No Regard for the Truth

NO REGARD FOR THE TRUTH

Friendship and kindness. Tragedy and injustice.
Rowville's Italian prisoners of war.

DARREN ARNOTT

Copyright © Darren Arnott 2019

All rights reserved. This book may not be reproduced in whole or part, stored, posted on the internet, or transmitted in any form or by any means, electronic, mechanical, photocopying, recording, or other, except brief extracts for the purpose of review, without written permission from the author of this book.

Front cover image: Photograph of Rodolfo Bartoli supplied by Nora O'Ryan. Bartoli, Rodolfo to Nora Gearon. 10 November 1945. Letter written from Mount Martha.

Back cover image: *The Truth*, 25 May 1946, p. 8, photograph of Captain Waterston *Department of Defence Co-Ordination Minute Paper*, 2 September 1946. Rowville Prisoner of War Hostel Report. NAA: MP742/1, 255-6-774 Part 1

Printed and bound in Australia by BookPOD

ISBN: 978-0-6486796-0-8

A catalogue record for this book is available from the National Library of Australia

'Captain Thomson, as I have stated, was the officer immediately in charge of Captain Waterston…and I have no hesitation in saying that he was a witness who had no regard for the truth.'

Justice Simpson
(Final Report into the Administration of the Rowville Prisoner of War Control Hostel and the circumstances resulting in the death of an Italian prisoner of war, No. 48833 R. Bartoli.)

Contents

	Preface	ix
Chapter 1	From Capture to Internment	1
Chapter 2	Italians in the Cowshed	9
Chapter 3	The Alleged Mistreatment of Prisoners	21
Chapter 4	He Has Killed Me!	25
Chapter 5	The Military Court of Inquiry – Foolishness and Larking	43
Chapter 6	The Homicide Squad Investigates	57
Chapter 7	Major Archer's Report – No Grounds for Complaint	65
Chapter 8	The Coroner's Inquest – the Shooting of Rodolfo	69
Chapter 9	A Veritable Nero – Justice Simpson's Inquiry Commences	83
Chapter 10	John Finn – Missing Iron Sheets and Stolen Goods	99
Chapter 11	Justice Simpson – Captain Thomson and Major Ruddock	107
Chapter 12	Justice Simpson – Inquiry Finding	127
Chapter 13	Courts Martial and Major Ruddock	141
Chapter 14	After Internment	159

Timeline of Events	171
Witnesses at Military Court of Inquiry	174
Witnesses Called at the Coroner's Inquest	175
Witnesses Called at Justice Simpson's Inquiry	176
Witnesses Called at Captain Waterston's Court Martial	180
Witnesses Called at Captain Thomson's Court Martial	181
Maps	182
Endnotes	183
Acknowledgements	197
About the Author	198

Preface

I grew up in Rowville during the 1970s and 1980s. As a child, I had heard stories of an army camp in Rowville. Australian soldiers, thousands of American Marines and, later, Italian prisoners of war had been stationed at the camp. Something that had always intrigued me was the Italian prisoners of war who had stayed there. I wondered what Italians were doing in Rowville. Why were they so far from home during World War Two?

I used to ride my pushbike around the dirt roads where the camp used to be and recall seeing the concrete foundations of the camp buildings. As the area developed, most of the roads and camp building foundations disappeared under a housing estate. In the late 1990s, we moved to a house in the area and there was a small bushland reserve just nearby. Within the reserve are the foundations of one of the buildings and I was reminded of the stories about the army camp. With archive facilities starting to be available online at the time, I did some searching. The first document I found was titled 'Shooting of Italian POW PWI 48833 – Rodolfo Bartoli at Rowville Prisoner of War Control Hostel'. I wondered, who was Rodolfo? Where had he come from? Why was he shot? I discovered that I could view these archive documents in Melbourne.

At the National Archives of Australia office in Melbourne, I was presented with two large archive boxes filled with documents. They contained government and military correspondence, transcripts of court cases and inquiries, and a folder with a title that captured my attention – 'Exhibits'. The exhibits folder contained the original camp diaries, an official map of the camp, hand-drawn maps and letters written by Italian internees and the police investigating the shooting. The court transcripts were lively documents and it was almost possible to feel present, listening to the banter in the courtroom as the camp staff and internees were being interviewed. The transcripts gave an insight into the Italians and their daily life in the camp.

Last year, I decided to focus on this story again and write this book. As I pieced together the course of events, stories emerged of violent assaults on prisoners, theft of property and a romance between a prisoner and a local Australian girl. As I read further, it became evident that the initial statement that the camp commandant gave to explain the shooting – that he was attempting to prevent the escape of an Italian prisoner – was clearly untrue. In telling this story, my hope is that Rodolfo's voice can be heard and that a light is shone on the injustice suffered by Rodolfo and those who cared for him.

Towards the end of my research for this book, I was extremely fortunate to be able to meet Nora O'Ryan (née Gearon) and Carmel Riddell (née Gearon) who both lived in Rowville at the time these events took place. The Italians were regular and welcome visitors to the Gearon farm and many of them became close friends. I am incredibly grateful for the personal stories, photos and letters that Nora and Carmel shared which have contributed to this book.

A note on dates and capitalisation. Dates and capitalisation included within quotes have been standardised for consistency.

Darren Arnott – May 2019

CHAPTER 1

From Capture to Internment

By 1946, when the events of this story take place, Italy had long since changed sides, joining the allied forces in the war against Nazi Germany. The war had ended and Italian prisoners who had been interned in Australia were waiting for ships to become available so they could return home. By this time, many of the prisoners had been away from their homes for six years.

At the request of the British Government, over 18,000 Italian soldiers, many of them captured in northern Africa and the Middle East, had been shipped to Australia. An employment scheme in Australia was implemented, allowing Italian prisoners to be employed helping with the labour shortage while many working Australian men were stationed overseas during the war. Prisoners were paid for their labour by the British Government. They received a partial payment from the Australian Government if they were being housed at their place of employment, such as prisoners living on farms. They also received a small payment and an allowance of cigarettes or tobacco from the Italian Government. Prisoners were paid in token money that could only be spent in canteens within the camps and hostels.[1]

The rights of the prisoners were protected by the Geneva Convention. Camp rules relating to the treatment of prisoners were drafted from the Geneva Convention by Major T McNeill Simpson. These rules were incorporated into a document known as National Security (Prisoner of War) Regulations and POW Camp Order No. 13.[2]

The Rowville hostel opened in December 1944 with 100 Italian prisoners. The hostel was under the supervision of the Murchison Control Centre which oversaw twenty-four camps or hostels. Only four of these camps were enclosed by wire. Thirteen of the camps housed prisoners who were employed on nearby farms and the remaining camps were hostels where prisoners were sent out to work without a guard. The Rowville camp was classified as a hostel and many of the men worked at the engineer's depot at the Oakleigh rail yards, the salvage depot at Fishermen's Bend or on farms in the area. In June 1945, the Rowville hostel became a staging camp or transition point where prisoners were to be placed while awaiting relocation to other posts around Victoria. It was also a destination for prisoners serving detention for minor offences. By August 1945, prisoner numbers had increased to 246, with one Australian officer and fifteen other ranks on staff to maintain the hostel and supervise the prisoners. From December 1944 to August 1946, over 2,600 Italian prisoners of war passed through the camp.[3]

The Rowville hostel was located on the south-west corner of Stud and Wellington roads and had originally been constructed as an army camp for Australian troops in 1942. It was later used by American Marines in 1944, prior to them being deployed to the Pacific Islands.[4] From December 1944, the camp was used as a hostel for Italian prisoners of war.

Rowville is twenty-seven kilometres south-east of Melbourne, located on the crossing of two main highways, Stud Road and Wellington Road. In 1946, Rowville was a small farming village, with the nearest major town being Dandenong, six kilometres away. Rowville is bounded by the Dandenong Creek to the south, the Dandenong Creek to the west, the Corhanwarrabul Creek to the north and the Lysterfield Hills to the east. The bridges across these creeks and the hills to the east marked the boundaries for prisoners; they weren't allowed beyond these points.

From Capture to Internment

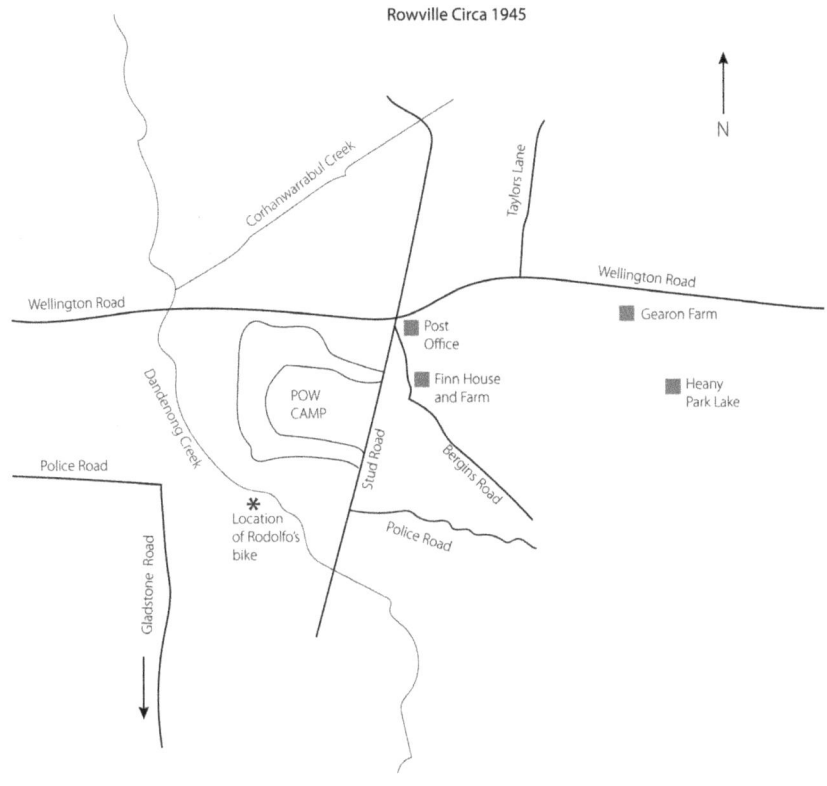

Rowville in 1945

The prisoners' daily routine in the camp consisted of getting up at 7 am for breakfast. The men would then assemble for a headcount before leaving by truck to their work sites. Men going out to work would leave on trucks by 9 am and would return to the hostel by 5 pm. There was an evening headcount with dinner at 6 pm, then a 10 pm rollcall and lights out. Prisoners wore burgundy-dyed uniforms supplied through the quartermaster store, which was run by one Australian military staff member with the assistance of an Italian prisoner, Rodolfo Bartoli. The Italians had their own cooks who would cook the meals each day so they were able to enjoy Italian food; camp ration documents show a good supply of spaghetti, macaroni and tomatoes.[5] Prisoners either slept in huts or in military-style tents, more of which were added to the camp as prisoner numbers grew. For recreation, the men used to play soccer, Australian Rules football and cards. There were two recreation huts, one of which was also used as a mess room in addition to a smaller mess room.

Brian Seymour Remembers

In 1945, Brian Seymour was a twelve-year-old schoolboy. Brian had grown up in a world devoid of men. His father, uncles and cousins were all at war. Brian's father Bob enlisted in 1939 and had seen action in Papua New Guinea where he was seriously wounded. Bob returned to Australia for medical treatment and towards the end of 1945 was posted to the Rowville Italian POW camp as the senior non-commissioned officer.

Brian was interviewed by Bryan Power for the *Rowville–Lysterfield Community News* in March 2004. Brian shared his memories of life in the camp, showing normal men a long way from their homes.

> Brian was keen to re-establish his bonds with his father and jumped at the chance to spend time with him at Rowville. On Saturday mornings, Brian would ride his bike [from his home] in East Malvern to Caulfield or Carnegie railway stations to catch the train to Dandenong. On the first occasion, his dad was there to meet him in the camp truck, but on subsequent visits he had to ride his bike out along Stud Road to the camp. He remembered the produce stalls outside the farmhouses in Stud Road in what is now the built-up area of Dandenong. Brian usually stayed overnight at the camp and slept on a stretcher in his father's room.
>
> The camp itself was heavily treed, with a long road stretching out from and circling back to the main gate. During Brian's time at the camp, there were no tents but a large number of huts, all with concrete floors. Captain Waterston, the commanding officer, told Brian's father that he intended buying the camp when it was eventually decommissioned and using it as a pig farm because the concrete slabs would make excellent bases for the sties.

The camp buildings along Stud Road in Rowville, 1945; other ranks' mess, kitchen and ration store[6]

Rowville Army Camp buildings, 1945; officers' mess and sergeants' mess

Rowville Army Camp buildings, 1945; administration building, quartermaster store, bulk and general-purpose store and drying hut

Brian remembers Captain Waterston as a big, red-faced man who slurred his words when he spoke. Brian only saw him when he (Brian) was at the camp on weekdays during the school holidays; he never saw him at the weekends. However, his own father only had leave occasionally while he was based at Rowville. Brian was not aware of the incident at the camp when Captain Waterston shot one of the internees. His father never spoke of it to him.

The perimeter fences were no more than you would find around a cow paddock – they certainly weren't built to keep anyone in. And there were no guards at the entrance, so anyone could walk in or out whenever they liked. Of course, the war was over and the only reason why the Italians were still there was because of the worldwide shortage of ships that resulted in their long wait for repatriation.

Brian often went for walks along the Rowville roads with his new friends, who were always dressed in army clothing that had been dyed a burgundy colour to identify them as POWs, and they never had to seek anyone's permission before leaving the camp. When they reached a certain point, they'd say, 'This is where we turn around' and they'd head back to the camp.

Another popular form of exercise was soccer and Brian was always invited to join them in their games when he visited the camp.

Brian's father, Bob, got on well with the prisoners and was quite happy for Brian to mingle with them. For their part, the prisoners were delighted to spend time with Brian. They all had that strong Italian love of family and Brian recalls being treated 'like a hero'. One young man, whose name was Pomponi, became a very good mate and took Brian under his wing, interpreting for him the Italian conversations going on around him so he would not feel left out. Pomponi had two young children back in Italy and he missed them very much.

Brian remembers the inmates as being fit and healthy young men. Those that he came to know had been farmers or craftsmen before being 'press-ganged' into the Italian Army and sent to fight in North Africa. Some of them had been captured before they'd had a chance to fire a shot and were happy to have survived the war and be living in Australia. Bob told Brian that he was sure that some of the POWs would abscond rather than be returned to Italy.

Brian often ate with them in the mess hut and enjoyed the typical Italian pasta meals that the prisoners themselves cooked. Many of them were sent out each day to work in market gardens and they'd come back with fresh vegetables that had been given to them by the farmers, so they were able to enjoy a healthy diet. One day, Brian had the thrill of going out in the back of the camp truck with one of the work gangs that had been assigned to harvest asparagus.

There was a canteen in the camp where internees could buy a variety of goods using their allowance of special internment camp coins. Brian's Italian friends could buy a number of things that weren't available in the normal shops in those days, including that wonderful luxury, chocolate. Brian was delighted when they shared this treat with him. Other examples of their generosity to Brian and his father are still in the possession of the family and include numerous documents and jewellery boxes with hidden openings, as well as several ships in bottles. All were made from materials found in the camp but are beautifully crafted. They made their own musical instruments too and, of course, being Italian, they loved to sing, which they would do quite spontaneously without any embarrassment.

Another form of entertainment were the movies that were shown on occasional Saturday nights. Brian remembers sitting in the crowded hut and feeling sorry for those who didn't understand English well enough to be able to really enjoy the movie. There was only one projector so there were several breaks in the show while the operator changed reels.

Brian looks back on those days as being a very happy time in his life. One of the lasting impressions his experiences at the Rowville camp had on him was that he has always, since then, considered Italians to be very nice people.[7]

The Italian prisoners were a common sight walking along the roads of Rowville during 1945 and 1946. They also left a lasting and positive impression on some of the families living in Rowville at the time. One of those families was the Gearon family.

CHAPTER 2

Italians in the Cowshed

The Gearon family farm was located by Wellington Road, one mile east of the camp. They were a family of eleven: John and Ada Gearon and their nine children, five boys and four girls. One of their sons, Pat, was serving in the Royal Australian Air Force and had been based in the Middle East. Edmond (Ted) ran a large poultry farm on the property.

John Gearon was the president of the Labor Party in Dandenong and, as a result, the family was knowledgeable about politics and political issues. This was helped by the fact that copies of Hansard were kept in the outhouse, serving a dual purpose. The Gearons were a musical family, regularly performing at dances and events in the local area and around Melbourne. One afternoon, in late 1944 or early 1945, two Italian prisoners wearing their red trousers wandered into John Gearon's cowshed and introduced themselves. John took them to the house to meet the family. When asked later about welcoming the Italian prisoners to his house, John said that he had a son serving in the Middle East and he hoped, if his son was ever unfortunate enough to be taken prisoner, that someone would welcome him just like John welcomed the Italians.

While the Italians were in Rowville, they were regularly at the Gearons' property helping on the farm, cutting hay and even doing some concreting around the house.

Italians from the camp cutting hay and making hay
bales at the Gearon farm in Rowville

The Italians were regular visitors on Sunday afternoons and evenings where they would play music, sing and play cards. They always left by 9 pm to return to the camp for the evening rollcall. Nora was twenty years old and Carmel was sixteen. They both remember the Italians being beautiful singers with magnificent voices. Ada, whom everyone called Mum, would cook cakes, biscuits and a Sunday evening meal for the prisoners who visited. Their father would always sit at the head of the crowded table. Carmel recalls that the Italians were around only about a year, but it made such an impact on the family. They learned about operas and other things that young farm girls wouldn't have had the opportunity to learn about. They taught them so much. Nora and Carmel both have fond memories of a shoemaker at the camp who made pairs of suede sandals for each of the four girls.

Lieutenant Dunt was in charge of the camp prior to Captain Waterston. Carmel remembers him being a lovely man who used to visit the Gearon farm to buy eggs. Three of the prisoners became very close friends: Giuseppe (Joe) Marchiafava, Eduardo Pizzi and Rodolfo Bartoli. Rodolfo, who was twenty-six years old, and Nora developed a romantic relationship. When together, they were always chaperoned by one of her brothers or her sister Carmel. Nora remembers Rodolfo being the tallest of the Italians with dark curly hair and a beautiful smile.

Rodolfo and Nora

Joe Marchiafava, Rodolfo Bartoli and unknown

Nora worked for the employment service in Melbourne during the week. Rodolfo would visit her sometimes after work or on the weekends. Some of the family later moved to a house in Dandenong and Rodolfo would ride a pushbike which he had hidden near the camp to visit Nora.

Carmel remembers Eduardo Pizzi being a beautiful artist who drew portraits of members of the family.[1]

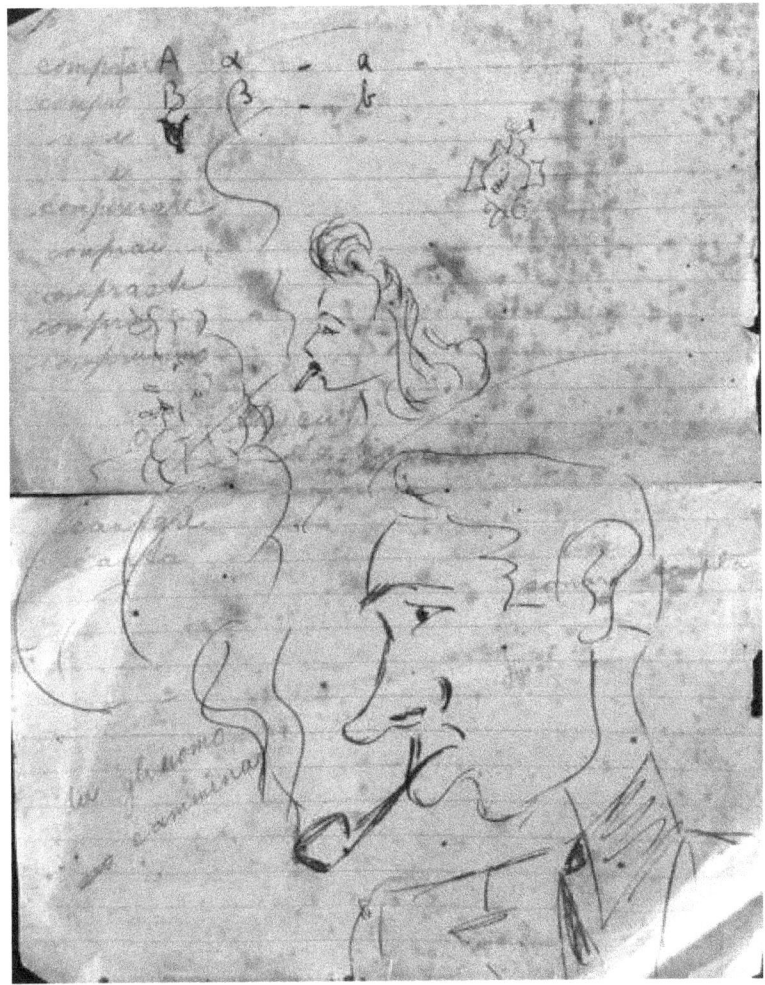

Some sketches of Eduardo's Italian-English lessons

Correspondence

Both Rodolfo and Eduardo spent time away from Rowville in late 1945. Rodolfo was at Koo Wee Rup for a short period of time and from late October 1945 both Rodolfo and Eduardo were interned at the Mount Martha camp.[2]

The 'National Security (Prisoner of War) Regulations and POW Camp Order No. 13 Part V – Communication by and with Prisoners of War' outlines the conditions under which prisoners could communicate with members of the public. Prisoners were required to use approved stationery supplied by the camp. Their letters were to be addressed including the recipient's full name and the prisoner's name and number on the back of the envelope. If the letter was written in a language other than English, it was to be clearly stated on the outside of the envelope – for example, 'letter written in Italian'. The letter from a prisoner was to be posted by the author of the letter by lodging it at a post box which was placed near the front gate of each compound.[3]

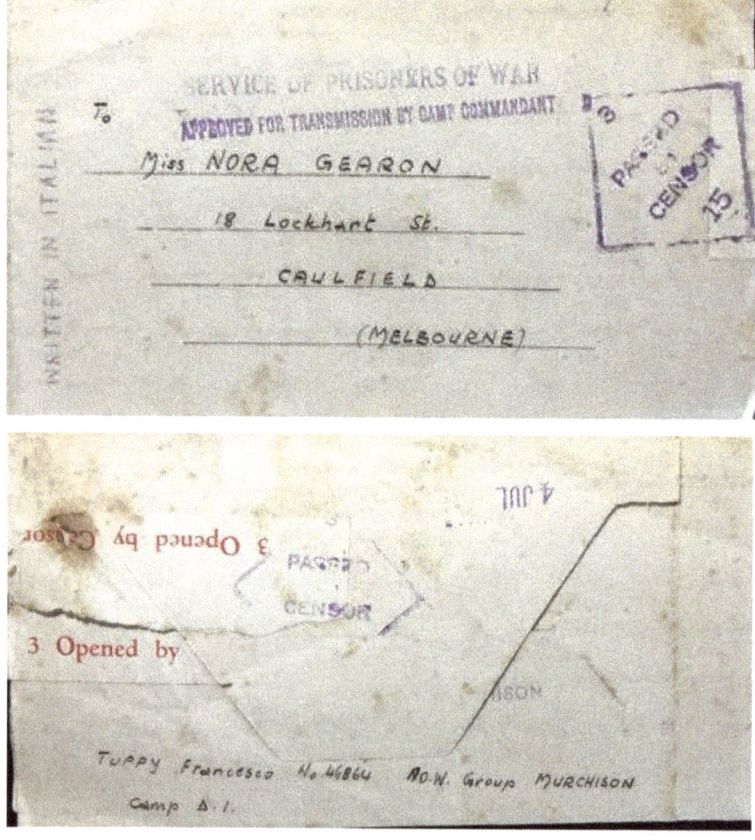

An example of a letter sent to Nora using approved POW Camp stationery

On his arrival at Koo Wee Rup on 5 October 1945, Rodolfo sent a letter to Nora written in Italian.

> Dear Nora,
>
> Pardon my lateness, but only today I was able to obtain an address where you can respond to my letters without any problems. Once again, I can taste all the bitterness of prison life! Far away from you, the days are terrible, long, gloomy and empty. I don't want to talk at length about my actual position, and it doesn't matter! It is sufficient for you to know that it's my hope to be able to once again be near you. It holds me back to take decisions and it spurs me to be patient. I anxiously await the return of the doctor of which I hope to obtain a big help so that my hope becomes reality (to return). Now let's talk a bit about us. Unfortunately, my insecurity of your language does not permit me to really know your sentiments towards me. Forgive me if my words are a bit harsh, but I love you so much and I would like to be sure of your affection to face with the tranquillity and adversity that will present in the future.
>
> I hope that you are as sincere as I am. Reflect on our reciprocal position; after this, will your sentiments be favourable toward me? I assure you that I will do all I can to not lose the trust that you have given me.
>
> Write to me soon because I need friendly words. Often, I think of the delicious hours that we spent together and the happiness that you were able to give me. All this makes me smile of hope and helps me put up with the solitude that I find myself in.
>
> I pray that you vividly thank your family for their hospitality and all that they did for me. Their goodness will always be in my memory. An eternal remembrance of gratitude to your mother. A particular thank you for the trust shown me. To all your sisters a thank you for the friendship and acceptance shown. A particular greeting to Carmela (I authorise you to kiss her for me). Respond to the address enclosed, putting the letter in double envelopes. Hoping that yours

will be the carrier of good news for me (for example a visit from you). How happy I would be if that was possible.

Receive my dear thoughts and infinite kisses

5 Oct 1945 Rodolfo

Rodolfo provided Nora with an address of a local farmer in the nearby town of Bayles for her to write back to, to avoid the official camp postal channels.

Rodolfo returned to Rowville four days later and was then transferred to Mount Martha on 16 October 1945. From there, Rodolfo wrote numerous letters to Nora. Some of the letters were written in English and some in Italian. When she received them, Nora met with an Italian woman in Melbourne to read the letters to her in English.

Just after arriving at Mount Martha, Rodolfo wrote a short letter to Nora telling her that he had been in Rowville a few days earlier but hadn't been able to see any of Nora's family. He said, 'I am always unlucky!' On 25 October, Rodolfo wrote to Nora and thanked her for arranging a bathing costume for him which he had requested and he writes about his affection for Nora.

> Accept my excuses which are sincere and hopefully soon I will cease being a number and soon gain my liberty. If I could send your letter to my mother with your good words, you would acquire her affection and acceptance. I hope that my imprisonment won't last much longer, and that I can really have the joy to see you again, she that up to a few months ago was the only person who made my life bearable…

> …many times I have told you that I like sincerity and I think I have shown you. I repeat myself, if I didn't really like you, it would cost me a lot. Now let's reciprocate with good heart our relationship, and this is the last thing I wish for, and why? Because I feel that you have with certainty commandeered my life. This is why I ask you to return in sincerity. We have a lot of difficulty to surpass, and only with a true

and profound love will it terminate with a victorious result, our proposal. Have you reflected at our difficulty and sacrifices we will encounter if within you persists the idea to unite your life with mine? I with your help am certain that we will be able to clear all the obstacles that will present, but for this I will need all your trust and love. Do you have the courage to unite with this silly guy?...

...In finishing, I return to think that today is Saturday and, not being with you, I content myself by going to bed and to relive the past, but always alive in my memory. In the Italian language, we do not use 'kiss me good night', and we don't have an equivalent word, therefore I send innumerable kisses and a big hug.

Your dearest Rodolfo

Eduardo wrote to Nora in English from Mount Martha with new instructions on how to secretly communicate with both Eduardo and Rodolfo.

Mount Martha
November 6

Dear Nora,

I am writing just a few lines to let you know about the new line of communication.

The person whose address I'm giving is fully trustworthy and, being well known in Mount Martha and a friend of the Postmaster, will receive without any trouble all the letters you would send him to this postal address: Robert Baker, Mount Martha.

I repeat, he is really to be trusted, being a kind, nice chap and, after all, I would never (as you will probably guess) let you take any chance whatsoever.

You will have to use two envelopes each time (you don't mind, do you?), writing on the inner my name (Rudolph doesn't know him) and, on the exterior, the above written address.

I will immediately recognise your handwriting (am I not marvellous!) and give it to that sweet pudding who is Rudy.

Remember me to all the family, giving my kindest regards to your mother.

Eduardo

Rodolfo continued to write to Nora regularly until his return to Rowville in late December 1945. On 21 December 1945, he wrote to Nora.

Darling,

Maybe tomorrow I am going to Rowville and perhaps after is somewhere else. Really, I don't know the reason but, in these cases I saw during my captivity, the good is waiting for me.

You can imagine how I am waiting for this. I love you and, thinking I have to wait so long time before I give you my news, I'm getting crazy.

If I'll be so lucky to see you at Rowville (it is just a dream), I'll let you know about myself; in the other case, if you'll be willing to wait for me, at the first occasion I'll send you my news.

Don't write to me anymore until I let you know where I am.

I thank your people once again for everything they did for me and I'll remember their kindness forever.

> Pardon me Nora if I were not able to tell you how I love you; believe me, I wish I were together with you to tell you what you are for me and if I couldn't with my words I should make you understand with my kisses –
> I'm going to close this letter. I don't want to say you good bye. I'm still hoping I'll see you again so I say you good night and thinking of you I kiss you – Rodolfo

One of Rodolfo's letters written in English to Nora

Rodolfo on the Gearon farm

While these were happy times, as friendships between the family and the Italians grew, the family began to become aware of some disturbing incidents at the camp and stories of some of the prisoners in the camp being brutally mistreated by the camp commandant.

CHAPTER 3

The Alleged Mistreatment of Prisoners

On 1 March 1946, a letter was sent to the Minister for Immigration, Arthur Calwell.

Dear Mr Calwell,

I would like to bring under your notice the following facts which have come to my ears. I know that these goings on are not in accordance with the policy of this country and will certainly rouse your indignation.

At the POW Camp at Springvale there is a certain Captain Waterston who is a veritable Nero. He is always drunk and treats the POWs shockingly. They are not free to have any possessions of their own, all articles of any value being taken out of their cases, such as shirts. He makes a clean sweep of anything they manage to purchase out of their small earnings, even to cigarette papers, razor blades, shirts, shoes.

Apparently, he gets intoxicated every day; then he goes around brandishing a revolver in mid-air. The prisoners are belted and given bread and water once a day and their money taken away from them whenever they attempt to escape because they cannot tolerate the conditions any longer. A few months ago, one man was taken to hospital and had to have seven stitches in his forehead. Several have gone out of their minds, and been taken to receiving homes.

The food is very scanty. In fact, they are all very unhappy. There seem to be a lot of Jews there. I have been told that these facts have been verified from various sources but it should be easy enough to have an inquiry. I was told also that this captain is a protected person, that is, someone with influence.

As this has been going on for some time, I would be happy if some move were to be made to end this state of affairs at the earliest possible moment, as it has caused a terrible lot of discontent.[1]

Thanking you,

I am,

Yours sincerely,

L Santospirito

The author of the letter was Louisa Angelina (Lena) Santospirito of Carlton. She was well known in the Australian Italian community as a charity worker and campaigner for the rights of Italian immigrants during and after the war. She was a founding member of the Archbishop's Committee for Italian Relief and was the Committee President from 1946 to 1954. The Committee was very active in the post-war years in dealing with the Department of Immigration on behalf of Italian immigrants and helping many Italian immigrants to find employment.

Arthur Calwell was the Minister for Immigration in March 1946 and was Mrs Santospirito's local Federal Member for the seat of Melbourne; he was also a personal friend. Mr Calwell assisted Mrs Santospirito in dealing with the Department of Immigration on many cases and this may have been a factor in the issue of the Rowville camp being escalated so quickly. Mrs Santospirito's work in helping the Italian community and her connections with the right people in parliament were mentioned in the Italian press in an article by Geno De Sanctis where he wrote: 'To locate Calwell, all it took was one phone call to an Italian in Melbourne, la Signora Santospirito, who they call here "la mamma degli italiani" (the mother of Italians).'[2]

Mrs Santospirito's letter triggered a chain of correspondence between the Minister for Immigration, the Minister for Army and the army itself.

On 21 March 1946, Mr Frank Sinclair, the Secretary to Mr Frank Forde, the Minister for Army, sent a letter to the Adjutant-General, outlining the allegations in Mrs Santospirito's letter and asking for the army to make inquires on behalf of the Minister.[3]

On 27 March, the Adjutant-General wrote to Southern Command Headquarters with a copy of Mrs Santospirito's letter of complaint and closed with the following request: 'It is desired that the above allegations be investigated immediately by your HQ and a full report on the position forwarded to HQ AMF in order that a reply may be furnished to the Minister as soon as possible.'[4]

Major Archer was appointed to head the army investigation. He was asked to report on all of the matters mentioned in the letter with a particular focus on the alleged drunkenness of Captain Waterston, the alleged physical ill-treatment of prisoners, the alleged confiscation of articles purchased by prisoners and the allegation that food was scanty.[5]

Major Archer's investigations had only just commenced when on a Saturday evening in March 1946, a tragic incident took place at the camp.

CHAPTER 4

He Has Killed Me!

AN ARTICLE IN *THE HERALD* ON MONDAY 18 FEBRUARY 1946 reads as follows:

5 Of 14 Escapees Caught
Fourteen enemy war prisoners escaped from detention centres in the weekend and five have been recaptured. In addition to the eight Italians who broke out of Rowville internment camp near Dandenong on Saturday, two more escapes there were reported by the army authorities today.

Outside Aid?
An Army report to the police says that the Saturday night break from Rowville was made by ripping up the floorboards of a guard house where the eight Italians were serving detention sentences. It is suspected that these men had outside assistance to aid their break for liberty, but no information was given by the Army to support that probability. None of the prisoners was under guard with the exception of Pexa, details of whose escape have not yet been learned. [Pexa was a German prisoner of war who escaped from Murchison on 18 February 1946.]

All were at control points on POW hostels and were 'on a sort of parole'. They are free to move almost unhindered over a radius of a mile from their headquarters. There is nothing to stop them going further and they took advantage of this liberty to escape. The only places where prisoners and internees are under guard are at

Myrtleford, Murchison and Tatura where they are in compounds behind barbed wire.

Descriptions

The men at large are-

From Rowville: –

Giuseppe Cappello, 26. 5ft 5in, stocky build, brown eyes, black, wavy hair, brown moustache, cleft chin.

Nazzareno Rosa, 27. 5ft 8in, medium build, brown eyes and hair.

Giuseppe Faccini, 29. 5ft 7in, brown eyes, dark hair.

(These men got away on Saturday night and were wearing burgundy prisoner-of-war clothing.)

Francesco Ponzoni, 35. 5ft 4in, slight build, brown hair and eyes.

Marino Benetti, 30. 5ft 7in, brown eyes, black hair. (Both these men speak English. They escaped between 11 pm yesterday and 7 am today. Both are believed to be wearing burgundy clothing and military boots.)

From Mount Martha: –

Isidoro Camaroto, 28. 5ft 10in, slight build, dark complexion, long brown hair, hazel eyes.

Francesco Goriziano, 31. 5ft 3in, medium build, dark hair and complexion brown eyes. Guido Iori, 32. 5ft 5in, slight build, hazel eyes, black hair. Speaks good English.

(All believed to be wearing burgundy clothing.)

Although the article states that eight prisoners escaped from Rowville that night, only five Rowville prisoners' names are included in the article. There is no record in the Rowville camp diary of who escaped that evening.

Some of the prisoners who escaped on 18 February 1946[1]

The camp diary contains entries recording fifteen instances of escapes since 18 February 1946 up until 30 March 1946, including the eight that escaped on 18 February. The entry in the Rowville camp diary for 4 March reads: 'Two POW escape during night from detention. Pizzi – Bianci. Reported to authorities.'[2]

Eduardo Pizzi, who was known for being argumentative with Australian soldiers and, as a result, finding himself in detention, was serving time in custody for being caught out of bounds by the commanding officer at the Mount Martha camp. He was sent to the Rowville hostel to serve his sentence. Eduardo was a student of classical studies, learning Greek and Latin, and spoke English very well. He spent time with the local Drummond family on their farm where they got to know him. He had told them that he had been captured in the Western Desert in North Africa by Australian forces when he was only eighteen. Eduardo was a member of a wealthy Roman family who owned the largest newspaper in Rome and his father had been a member of Mussolini's cabinet.[3] While being interviewed at Justice Simpson's inquiry, Eduardo complained about the food in the camp, especially breakfast, which consisted of a military pannikin full of milk and tea or white coffee and a slice of bread. Eduardo said that he often had to buy his own food because he was so hungry. When asked what a usual breakfast was for him at home, he said that he usually would have eggs, bacon and some coffee and then a second breakfast at 10 am. Mr Minogue asked Eduardo how much he currently weighed, and he answered, 175 pounds (79 kg). Mr Minogue then told Justice Simpson that Eduardo had weighed 142 pounds (64 kg) when he first arrived in Australia. Justice Simpson responded, 'I think I can save you a little trouble. Nobody is going to suggest that this gentleman is dying from starvation.'[4]

On 4 March 1946, while in detention at Rowville, Eduardo escaped from the guardroom by, allegedly, breaking the door. He was recaptured sometime later and, while giving evidence at Justice Simpson's inquiry, he explained that when he escaped from Rowville, he didn't break the door; he had simply unscrewed the screws and bolts on the door and walked out. After one of his escapes, Ada Gearon found Eduardo asleep in their house in Dandenong.[5] He wasn't recaptured until close to Christmas later that year while he was doing his Christmas shopping in a city store. The two detectives who captured him noted that he was wearing a new brown double-breasted suit when he was apprehended.[6]

Eduardo working for the Drummond family in Rowville[7]

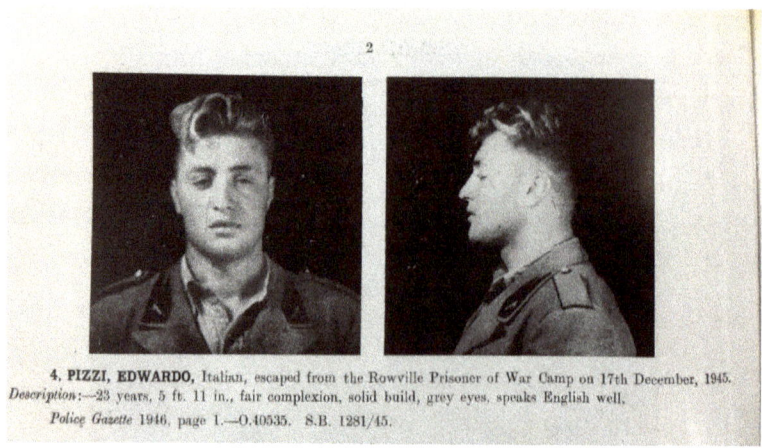

Eduardo Pizzi in the *Police Gazette*[8]

One of the eight prisoners who escaped on the evening of 18 February was Francesco (Frank) Ponzoni. Frank had met a young Australian girl, June Peterson, at the nearby Heany Park Lake, a popular swimming spot. They struck up a relationship and Frank got to know June and her family well. Frank, like many of the prisoners in the camp, was bored and frustrated with the delay in being returned home. June's family devised a plan to assist Frank to escape from the camp. At midnight, June's mother and father drove out to the camp and met Frank at a prearranged location. They not only assisted him to escape but also provided him with accommodation and employment. In an attempt to conceal his identity, Frank shaved off his moustache and wore glasses. He worked with June's father as a painter-decorator until he was recaptured over twelve months later. Frank married June in September 1947. They were married for forty-three years until Frank passed away in 1990.[9]

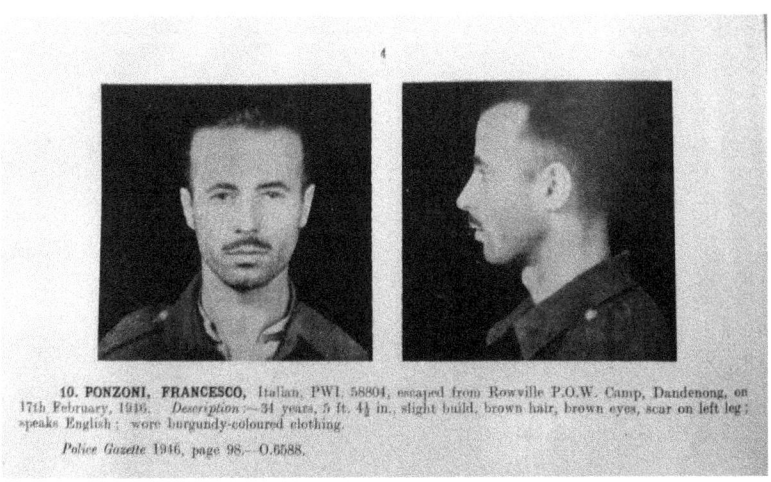

Francesco Ponzoni in the *Police Gazette*[10]

Under the Wire

Almost six weeks after Frank Ponzoni's escape, at 6.48 pm on Saturday 30 March, the Victoria Police Communications Centre, D24, received a phone call from Camp Commandant Captain Waterston, requesting assistance at the camp. A call was broadcast to police cars in the area.

> 'Camp reports trouble among POWs Requests that patrol be sent to assist. Contact Sergeant and Police on duty in street and instruct them to attend.'
>
> Radio broadcast from Lieutenant Maloney: 'I will go to Rowville, please detail Sergeant Carroll in car 116 to attend and take any action necessary pending my arrival.'[11]

Around 6.30 that evening, as most prisoners were finishing their evening meal, Rodolfo Bartoli suffered a serious gunshot wound. Nearby prisoners who heard the gunshot and Rodolfo's cries of 'he has killed me' ran to his aid. Rodolfo was carried to the camp hospital on a stretcher where he was treated by the Italian camp doctor, Giuseppe (Joseph) Galli. Rodolfo was losing a great deal of blood and Doctor Galli, realising that Bartoli's condition was quickly deteriorating, called for a camp car to rush Rodolfo to the Heidelberg Military Hospital.[12]

Constable McAvoy, Constable Banks and Constable Hodge were the first police officers to arrive at the camp, shortly after receiving the call over the radio. They met Captain Waterston. Constable McAvoy documented in his notebook his brief conversation with Captain Waterston.

He asked Captain Waterston, 'What is the trouble, sir?'

'There has been some trouble here tonight. I threw a picket around the camp. I was walking through the camp myself when I saw a man moving through the wire. I called on him to stop and he did not stop. I then fired a shot. Later I found that a man had been injured in the groin, or shot in the groin, and he had been sent to the Heidelberg Military Hospital.'

'Do you want us to do anything now?'

'I would like you to come down with me around the camp. I am short-staffed here.'

Constables McAvoy, Banks and Hodge walked with the captain and the Italian interpreter through the camp. The captain ordered a number of prisoners who were walking around to return back to their huts. The camp was quietened down and all lights were turned out.

The captain and the three policemen returned to the captain's office where they were met by the provost (military police) with seven men, an officer and Sergeant McPhee from Dandenong Police Station. Constable McAvoy's main concern that evening was addressing the nature of the call they had received, the suspected trouble and possible uprising. They were not investigating the shooting and at the time considered this to be a military matter. Had Rodolfo died while they were there, the homicide squad would have been called. Constable

McAvoy and his colleagues stayed at the camp for about twenty minutes. They observed that everything seemed to be under control, so the constables returned to the city to continue their general patrol duties.

Before leaving, Constable McAvoy used the phone in Captain Waterston's office to provide a short report to D24. 'Captain Waterston VX5230, OC of the camp reports a "rising" among the POW tonight. Pickets were thrown around the camp to prevent any escapes and one Rodolfo Bartoli, 48833, who attempted to get away under the wire was shot in the groin by Captain Waterston. Remainder put to bed and lights put out. All normal now. Sergeant McPhee present also Lieutenant Maloney and 7th Provost arrived.'[13]

While the police and military police were attending to the situation at the camp in Rowville, Rodolfo was receiving treatment at the Heidelberg Military Hospital. Upon arrival there, he was resuscitated, given a blood transfusion and underwent surgery. Despite these efforts, he died at 11.30 that evening.

Later that evening, Captain Waterston told Doctor Galli, camp leader Michele Scuma and the camp padre to pack up their belongings as they would be relocated to other camps at 8 am the following morning.

The entry in the camp diary for 30 March reads:

> Routine patrols. PWI acting suspiciously. Appear to be getting food. Possible escapes. Attempting an escape at 1900 hrs PWI Bartoli was shot by PWCO. PWI Melampo escaped. Threats by PWI Galli and Camp Leader Scuma led to request by PWCO for reinforcements. Police patrols and Military Police assisted in quietening camp. No further trouble or escapes anticipated.

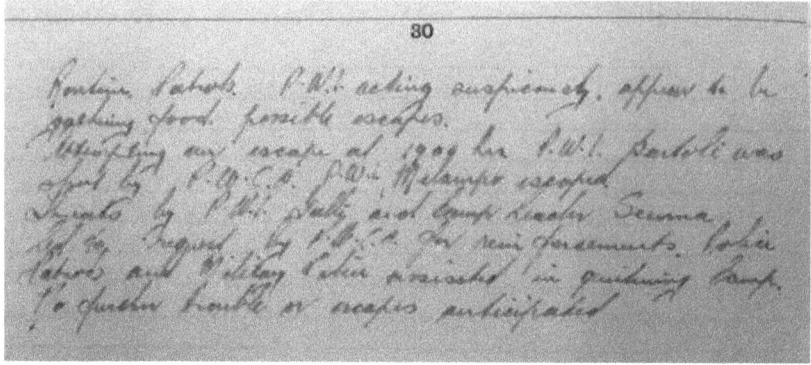

The entry for Sunday 31 March 1946 reads:

> Guards patrolling area. No trouble expected. Detective Howard visited camp at 1400 hrs in connection with shooting. Viewed area and boundaries. Two women reported attempting to entice PW out of camp. These were not apprehended.[14]

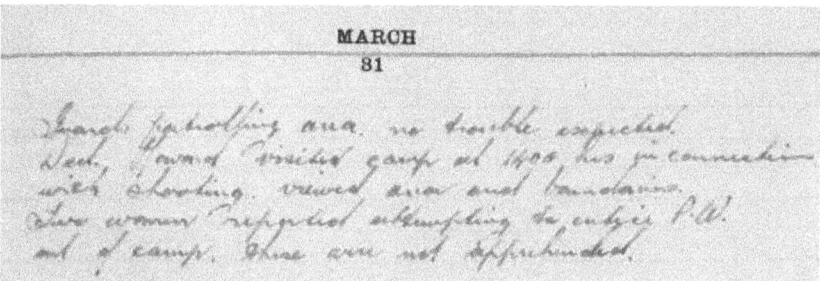

On Monday, 1 April, several newspapers reported a statement from the Coroner and the military, stating that the Coroner would be holding an inquiry and that there would also be a Military Court of Inquiry into the shooting. They provided some further details of Saturday night's events, along with a photograph of two armed soldiers searching for Melampo who had escaped that evening.

The Herald reported on Monday 1 April 1946:

> **Army Explains POW Shooting Case**
> Resentment by Italian war prisoners at being brought back to internment from farm work is believed to have caused a riot at

He Has Killed Me!

Rowville detention camp on Saturday night, when one prisoner was mortally wounded trying to escape.

There was much trouble at this camp last week. Guards were increased and military and civil police were rushed to Rowville on Saturday night to quell the disturbance. Only one prisoner is reported to have escaped.

The City Coroner (Mr Warwick PM) will hold an inquiry into the death of the Italian who was shot, Rodolfo Bartoli. He died from a bullet wound in the groin. Army accounts of the shooting discount any suggestion that a mutiny threatened. An army spokesman said today that evidence would be given at the court of inquiry that there was no concerted move by the prisoners, and that the shooting of Bartoli was an accident, due to the firing of a warning shot in the uncertain light. The inquiry would be a routine military one and would not be open to press or public. No date had yet been fixed for it.

Facts relating to the incident were that on Saturday afternoon several prisoners of war were seen to be acting furtively. They were whispering in a group and would stop talking when guards approached. Because of the suspicion that something was brewing the 11 guards stationed with the prisoners of war were placed on duty around the headquarters section of the hostel area. At 6.30 pm, the commandant of the camp (Captain J W Waterston) saw an Italian prisoner of war, Bartoli, trying to crawl under a wire fence, apparently trying to escape.

Uncertain Light

He called on him three times to halt and then fired a warning shot. Bartoli did not stop and Captain Waterston fired a second shot. It was aimed in front of the POW and intended as a further warning. In the uncertain light the shot hit Bartoli in the groin causing a wound from which the Italian later died. The Army spokesman said that there was no knowledge of any mass attempt by the POWs to escape although several had apparently been appearing to do so and one had got away in the excitement following the shooting.

After the shooting there was some murmuring among the prisoners but when they were ordered to their quarters and a curfew imposed the POWs went quietly. Police and other military personnel were called to the hostel. Twenty-two Italians have escaped from Rowville since December and twenty-eight are still at large from this and other detention centres in Victoria.

ARMED with pistols and rifles, Army men searched the Dandenong district today for Luigi Melampo, an Italian prisoner-of-war, who escaped from Rowville Camp on Saturday night. In that disturbance another P.O.W. was shot fatally while trying to escape.

The photo caption reads: 'Armed with pistols and rifles, Army men searched the Dandenong district today for Luigi Melampo, an Italian prisoner-of-war who escaped from Rowville Camp on Saturday night. In that disturbance, another POW was shot fatally while trying to escape.'15

> **ALIENS.**
>
> *Members of the Force gaining any information in respect to the matter published under this heading are to communicate such information immediately to Detective Sub-Inspector Birch, Special Branch, C.I.B., Russell-street, Telephone F6225 (direct **line**), and Russell-street, Extension 234 and 296, in addition to the usual supplementary Modus Operandi reports required.*
>
> **MELAMPO, LUIGI,** an Italian prisoner of war, escaped from Rowville Camp, Dandenong, on 30th March, 1946.— Description:—No. 61499, 25 years, 5 ft. 8 in., brown hair, grey eyes, dark complexion, slight build; wore burgundy-colour clothing, military boots. O.11407

Post in the *Victoria Police Gazette* about Luigi Melampo's escape[16]

Major Archer's investigation into the allegations made by Mrs Santospirito was already underway when the shooting took place. The news of the shooting in the press prompted Minister Forde to instigate a formal independent inquiry into the allegations and to include an investigation into the shooting.

On Monday 1 April, Mr Sinclair sent a memo to Minister Forde along with some press cuttings from the Monday newspapers about the shooting at the Rowville camp on Saturday night. Some of the press articles had suggested that there had been a mutiny in the camp on the night of the shooting. The memo was titled 'POW Camp – Rowville'.

> Minister: Herewith is the file dealing with the representations made to you by the Minister for Information and Immigration (Mr Calwell), together with the press cuttings dealing with the shooting of an Italian prisoner of war by the commanding officer, Captain Waterston.
>
> If the incident in regard to the shooting of the prisoner of war is read in conjunction with the allegations made by Mr [sic] Santospirito

regarding this camp, it gives the incidents associated with the shooting of the prisoner of war on 31 March [sic] rather a sinister appearance. However, it is, in my view, undesirable that you as Minister for the Army assume that Captain Waterston is – because of the latter event – guilty of all the misdemeanours outlined in Mr [sic] Santospirito's letter; nor do I consider that Captain Waterston should, on the evidence at present available, be suspended from duty unless the Adjutant-General is communicated with and his advice as to such action is sought.

In view of the allegations made by Mr [sic] Santospirito and of the incidents which led up to the shooting by Captain Waterston of the Italian prisoner of war who, it is alleged, was attempting to escape, the holding of an investigation independent of the Army – which has been suggested to you – would, I think, in all the circumstances be justified, particularly as such an investigation would sift out the true facts, and if these are in favour of the Camp Administration, can do neither the Commanding Officer nor the Army authorities any harm, while on the other hand if there is any truth in the allegations it is desirable that the Government should have the facts and be in a position to meet any criticism that may subsequently arise either from within Australia or the Italian Government.[17]

On the same day, Sinclair, the Secretary for the Minister for Army, wrote to the Adjutant-General:

The Minister referred me to the reference in the daily press today to a mutiny which occurred at the Rowville prisoner of war camp, near Dandenong which culminated in the fatal shooting of a prisoner of war by Captain Waterston, Camp Commandant.

The Minister referred me to representations received by him from a Ministerial source on 21 March containing serious allegations against Captain Waterston and asked that you should furnish advice at the earliest possible date of the result of investigations made on these allegations and on the investigations into the cause of the mutiny and the resultant death of a prisoner of war.[18]

A handwritten note from Minister Forde to Sinclair on 2 April reads:

> Mr Sinclair, please prepare suitable terms of reference for Mr Justice Simpson's inquiry into the POW camp administration at Rowville. I will then submit the draft to Dr Evatt.[19]

On 8 April 1946, Minister Forde announced in the House of Representatives the appointment of Justice Simpson to make an immediate investigation into the affairs of the camp and into the circumstances that led to the shooting with fatal results of an Italian prisoner of war on 30 March.

An outrageous article was printed in *The Truth* on Saturday 6 April, one week after the shooting. The full-page article featured photographs of nineteen prisoners, including Frank Ponzoni and Eduardo Pizzi. The article opened with the following headline and paragraph:

> **Break-out By 5000 Planned**
> **Italian POW Mutiny That Fizzed Out**
> Behind the planned mutiny at Rowville POW camp last weekend, which resulted in the fatal shooting of one Italian, was a scheme by which Italian prisoners-of-war at each of three main camps – Murchison, Hume and Rowville – would break free and scatter under a well-organised plan which provided for specially placed cars picking up escapees most desired by Australia's underground Fascist movement. Those not picked up by cars were to be secreted by Italian communities and either hidden, or 'passed on' until they were out of danger. But the plan misfired. The Rowville mutiny was premature. By the time Rowville's meagre guard was reinforced by civilian and military police, other POW camps harbouring Italians had been advised and they, too, were on the alert. The scheme collapsed – and it involved 5000 Italians!

The Truth, April 4 1946[20]

Nora didn't hear the news of Rodolfo's death until the Monday morning after the shooting, 1 April. She was travelling to work and met her sister Margaret on the train platform. Margaret had read the details of the shooting in the newspaper and told Nora: 'Rudolf's been killed.' Shocked and devastated, Nora didn't go to work that day and returned home.[21]

Romano Papina, a good friend of Rodolfo's who was in the same military unit as Rodolfo and was a family friend of the Bartolis, wrote to Rodolfo's brother to inform the family of Rodolfo's death. He also posted the family some photographs that Rodolfo had among his belongings.[22]

In response to Romano's letter, Rodolfo's father, Donatello Bartoli, wrote to Nora on 6 May 1946.

He Has Killed Me!

Miss Nora Gearon

Dear Nora:

You may easily understand how we have been struck by the terrible news of our dear Rodolfo's death! As we know how dearly you loved each other, you will be good enough to write us some details about the accident that has caused his death.

We have been informed by his friend Papina, whom you may also know for they were always together. This Papina wrote to his brother and the latter has cautiously informed my wife and me.

Although very likely we shall never meet, as would have been the case if you had married, I am sure you will sympathise with us, his parents, who have been so terribly struck by the disaster. In one of his late letters, Rodolfo spoke very nicely of you and we were quite glad you had met and were going to be married in due time. Destiny has willed that this should not be and so both we and you are bereaved by the death of our beloved Rodolfo.

If you have some of his photos or papers that you think would be of comfort to his poor mother and to myself, please send them to us. Write us as soon as you can; you may write in English for I am having this written by a friend of mine who is thorough in the language.

Hoping to hear from you and that you may be consoled by time of the great loss we have all suffered. I send you our best thoughts of sympathy.

Very lovingly yours,

Donatello Bartoli

Rodolfo was buried at the Springvale cemetery on 2 April 1946. The Gearon family was not aware of there being any ceremony or memorial for Rodolfo; however, Nora remembers going to visit the Springvale cemetery and later taking a photograph of the plaque with Rodolfo's name. The Gearon family continued corresponding with the Bartoli family and sent them food parcels.

Very kind Miss Nora,

In your dear letter dated Nov. 6th, I hear that my dear Rodolfo rest in a private tomb in Catholic cemetery. Believe me, Miss, that for a mother, to know that good people busy themselves of the tomb of her son is a great consolation, more because I cannot go to pray and cry where rest he who I loved so much. I am begging you a great favour: if you could send me a photograph of the tomb, I shall always be grateful to you and my Rodolfo will bless you from heaven.

I thank you very much for what you do for us, for the packets you send us and which we need much. You should like to know what we need but our need is so great that all what you will send will be useful for us and of great comfort.

Regards from my family to you and your good family. I send you my best wishes and a kiss.

Donatello Bartoli

CHAPTER 5

The Military Court of Inquiry – Foolishness and Larking

THE MILITARY COURT OF INQUIRY COMMENCED ON FRIDAY 5 April. The inquiry was held at the Rowville camp with the purpose of 'inquiring into and reporting upon the circumstances of the injuries sustained by PWI 48833 Bartoli Rodolfo on 30 March 1946, death of said PWI on 30 March 1946.'

The inquiry was presided over by Colonel Christison. Nine witnesses were heard: four military personnel, the military doctor who treated Rodolfo at the hospital and four of the prisoners. The inquiry commenced at 9.15 am with the court inspecting the camp and the location of the incident.

Captain Waterston was the first witness called and he gave an account of his version of events that evening.

There had been a total of twelve staff on duty at the camp that evening. During the late afternoon, Captain Waterston caught two prisoners taking lettuces from the engineer's vegetable garden. The captain questioned, searched and detained the prisoners. He suspected that there was going to be an attempted escape that evening. At the evening meal time, he armed two members of the staff and sent them to positions on Stud Road. Captain Waterston armed himself with a .303 rifle and Sergeant Major McDougall with a .38 pistol. Waterston instructed three staff to remain in the orderly room to attend to telephone duties and to draw arms from the arms chest if required.

Waterston explained. 'At approximately 1830 hours on the evening of 30 March 1946, I posted two guards in Stud Road. Then myself and Sergeant Major McDougall went to the south boundary of the camp and patrolled that area for the purpose of preventing PWI escaping.

'At approximately 1900 hours, I saw a prisoner running for the south boundary fence. I called on him to stop. He changed his course and ran at an angle towards the scrub in a westerly direction. I ran along the boundary fence, and again called on the prisoner to stop. He kept running, and I fired a shot over his head. He did not stop, and attempting to stop him reaching the scrub, I fired another shot at his ankles. The PWI then fell, and on investigation made later, it was found that he was shot. Sergeant Major McDougall came running from the scrub, and I had ascertained by that time that the prisoner was hit. I immediately dispatched the Sergeant Major for the doctor and stretcher bearers. I went to the office and rang Heidelberg for an ambulance. I was then informed by the POW doctor that the POW should be taken to hospital immediately. He was sent in a hostel staff car and arrived at the Heidelberg Military Hospital at 1935 hours. The prisoner of war concerned was PWI 48833, Bartoli, Rodolfo.'

The captain was then questioned by the court.

'How many times did you challenge this man before you fired?'
'Either two or three.'

'Was the shot fired from a rifle or a pistol?'
'From a rifle.'

The questioning continued around the likelihood of prisoners being armed with knives and then on to the topic of why the captain thought that there might be a break-out that night and why he felt the need to deploy patrols.

The Military Court of Inquiry – Foolishness and Larking

'Had you received any information that there was likely to be a breakout on this night?'
'I had received no information, but observation of the camp and the actions of certain PWI all pointed to an attempt that night to escape.'

'What observations had been made that prompted you to think that such an occurrence might happen?'
'I saw several prisoners getting into the scrub and carrying bread and jam. On further patrolling of the camp, I arrested two PWI with a bag of lettuce stolen from the engineer's garden.'

The captain was then asked about the boundaries of the camp.

'What are considered the boundaries outside which the PWI are not permitted to go?'
'The roadway at the south end of the camp.'

Captain Waterston explained that the prisoners were informed about the camp boundaries through notices and maps posted in the mess room. They were also given verbal instructions from the camp leader at the evening mess parades for those prisoners who couldn't read or write. Instructions had been given in both English and Italian at least once a week since the escapes on 18 February 1946. Prisoners were instructed that if they were seen outside of these boundaries that they would be treated as escapees and liable to be fired upon.

'Were you in the camp all day?'
'I was away for approximately two hours.'

'Where were you during that two hours?'
'First at the Dandenong Police Station. I was there approximately an hour, walked into Dandenong, did some shopping, had several drinks and returned to the camp. I went in at 1100 hours and returned to the camp at approximately 1300 hours. I did not leave the camp again.'

'Were you convinced that the prisoner was trying to escape?'

'I am positive of it.'

'What was the condition of visibility at that period?'
'Very bad, just on dark.'

Sergeant Major McDougall gave a similar account of events. 'On the evening of 30 March 1946 after 1800 hours, Captain Waterston and myself proceeded to the lower or southern end of the hostel boundary, and I was ordered to watch the south-western end. After being there approximately twenty minutes, I heard Captain Waterston call out what appeared to me to be a challenge. He called out twice, and then I heard a shot, then after a pause, another shot. After the second shot I moved quickly in the direction of Captain Waterston. When I saw Captain Waterston, he saw me approaching and he sang out, "The prisoner has been shot, bring the doctor and the stretcher bearers." I immediately ran to the hospital and informed the doctor, and he told the RAP [Regimental Aid Post, camp hospital] orderly and his assistant, and on the way out, the doctor said to me, "The captain forgets that we are two hundred strong." I then gave the doctor a direction, and I then moved down a little way in the direction of the southern boundary, and then back to the headquarters.'

The two Italian prisoners, Enrico Veronelli and Rosario Schirinzi, who carried Rodolfo on the stretcher to the camp hospital were questioned. They were both only asked two questions by the court.

'Did the Sergeant Major go right down to the spot where the body was?' They both answered no and said that he had pointed it out to them.

They were then shown a plan of the camp and asked to mark on the plan where they picked Rodolfo up from. They marked an 'x' on the map to show the position, on the centre of the map next to their handwritten names.

The Military Court of Inquiry – Foolishness and Larking

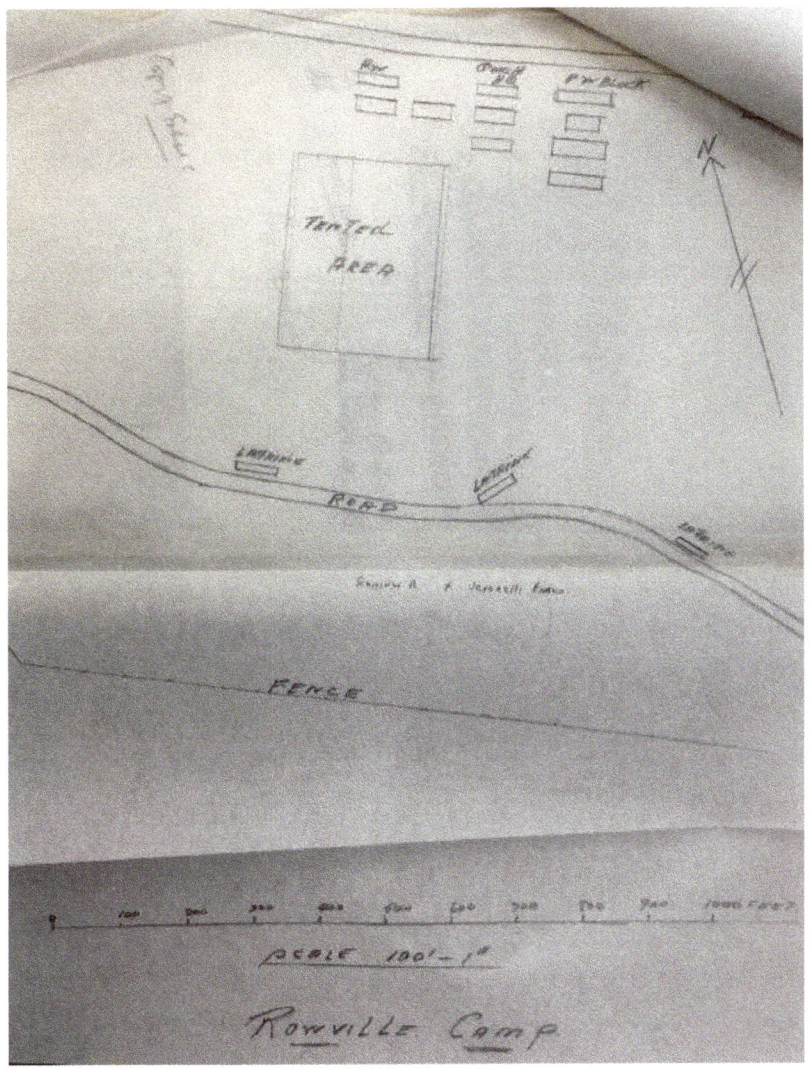

The map used by Veronelli and Schirinzi to show where they found Rodolfo[1]

When Doctor Galli, the Italian camp doctor, appeared at the inquiry, he was asked what action he took when he had been informed that a man had been shot.

He answered, 'I was informed by the Sergeant Major that a man had been shot and I went with him to the carpenter's shop which is about thirty-eight yards from the RAP. I remember telling the Sergeant Major that I thought this was too much, referring to the shooting of a man. When I got to the carpenter's shop I was taken with a feeling of disgust and I came back. I did not go down to the man who had been shot. I then came back to the RAP.'

Rodolfo was brought in about five minutes later. The doctor found that he was bleeding profusely and could see a hole in his right groin where a bullet had entered and a larger hole on his left buttock where the bullet had exited his body. Rodolfo had a very weak pulse and was complaining of abdominal pain. Doctor Galli realised that Rodolfo's condition was serious and went to Captain Waterston's office to check that an ambulance was on the way.

As Doctor Galli was leaving the office, Scuma arrived. Galli recounted overhearing Scuma talking to Captain Waterston. He could hear Scuma saying, 'I have to congratulate with you, Captain, for you—'. At this point, Doctor Galli walked into the office and said, also in a sarcastic tone, 'Me too, Captain, I have to congratulate you.' The captain said to Doctor Galli, 'You too, Doctor?' and pointed at Doctor Galli. Galli said, 'Keep down your hands, Captain. You can't treat me as you have been treating the other soldiers.' Galli informed the captain that he wanted to speak to a superior officer the next day.

Galli returned to the RAP to find fifteen prisoners waiting outside, many of them crying. Galli dressed Rodolfo's wounds and then sent the camp leader to Captain Waterston to fetch a car to take Rodolfo directly to the hospital. Galli, Scuma and a friend of Rodolfo's went to the hospital with him.

The Military Court of Inquiry – Foolishness and Larking

At 8 am the next morning, Captain Waterston told Galli to pack up his belongings and to be prepared to leave the camp at any time.

Michele Scuma, the camp leader at the time of the shooting, was asked if he went to the place where Rodolfo had been shot and was asked to show the location on a plan of the camp. He was also asked if it was his duty to inform prisoners of the camp rules and boundaries, to which he replied yes. He was asked if he was at the camp on 18 February when a number of men had escaped. He answered that he was.

'After that episode, were you told by the Commandant that any man who attempted to escape or assisted others in escaping would be fired at?'
'Not at that specific time, but at other times, the Commandant told me that any man found outside the road would be fired upon.'

'Did you convey that to the other prisoners of war?'
'No.'

'Do you think it was your duty to do so?'
'I did not think it a serious warning.'

'Did you speak to Captain Thomson this morning and use the expression "shot like a rabbit"?'
'Yes, sir.'

'Did the prisoners of war know that if they attempted to escape, they would be fired on?'
'In a closed camp with guards.' Unlike other camps, the Rowville camp was not a closed camp with guards.

Captain Thomson, Captain Waterston's immediate superior officer, and Lieutenant Purbrick both related a similar story that, earlier in the day of the Military Court of Inquiry, they had taken Scuma to the location of the shooting and questioned him about the camp boundaries. They both said that he was evasive initially but eventually agreed that the camp boundary was the southern fence until dark, at which time the southern road became the camp boundary. According to Captain Thomson, Scuma initially said that he hadn't told prisoners this but later said that the prisoners understood. From Captain Thomson's statement, 'Scuma attempted to evade my questions, but later admitted that he, as camp leader, had been warned that if prisoners of war were detected apparently trying to escape, shots were liable to be fired. PWI Scuma, to quote his own words, said "Shoot PWI like rabbits."'

More is revealed about Scuma's morning encounter with Thomson and Purbrick during Justice Simpson's inquiry several months later. Scuma recalls being driven down to the area where Rodolfo was shot. Captain Thomson had pointed to the southern road and said, 'Is this not the boundary after dark, yes?' Scuma replied, telling Thomson that the boundary was the fence. Thomson then asked Scuma what was to happen to a prisoner who attempted to escape. Scuma's reply was, 'It is not right to shoot a man like a rabbit. You can punish him by putting him into detention.' Scuma reinforced that Rowville is not a closed camp with gates and guards and that prisoners can simply walk out.

The final witness heard was Doctor Wales who had treated Rodolfo at Heidelberg Military Hospital. Doctor Wales explained that he treated Rodolfo at 2015 hours on 30 March 1946. Rodolfo had a perforating gunshot wound to the lower abdomen. There were two wounds: one above the right groin and the second in the left buttock. Rodolfo was resuscitated and operated on but, despite active treatment, he died at about 2330 hours.

The court asked Doctor Wales two questions.

'Had there been, in your opinion, any treatment prior to the patient's arrival at the hospital?'
'Yes, the left buttock was bandaged prior to arrival.'

'What was the cause of the PWI's death?'

'In my opinion, it was wholly caused by the gunshot wound above described.'

Final Report

In the final report from the Military Court of Inquiry, the court found that Rodolfo had died from a gunshot wound to the groin. He received the wound while trying to escape and while outside the camp boundary. The prisoner understood English and the captain had twice called for him to halt. The orders to halt were ignored. The captain fired a warning shot. The prisoner did not stop so the captain fired a second shot, also intended as a warning. In the failing light, the captain had fired higher than intended and the bullet hit the prisoner.

The court found the evidence on the subject of camp boundaries warnings to prisoners was conflicting. Captain Waterston stated that, since the escapes in February, he had told Scuma that the camp boundary after dark was the southern road. Captain Thomson and Lieutenant Purbrick stated that, on 5 April, Scuma told them that all the prisoners understood that they would be 'shot like rabbits' if they attempted to escape. The report states that, based on Scuma's observed demeanour when giving evidence, he was an evasive witness. Quoting directly from the report, 'It was particularly noted that he remembered having used the phrase "shot like the rabbit" to Captain Thomson and Lieutenant Purbrick but could not remember the remainder of the conversation, although it had only taken place that morning.'

The court found that the injury to, and death of, Rodolfo resulted from his own misconduct, in that he attempted to escape and failed to halt when challenged. It was also found that there was no breach of international convention relating to the treatment of POWs. It is particularly noted that two warnings were given before any shots were fired.

Immediately after the injury, the camp staff did everything in their power to give Rodolfo the best medical attention available. The court was of the opinion that the conduct of Galli merited severe censure in that he firstly neglected to attend to the injured man at the place where he received his injury, and, secondly, he wasted time making insubordinate remarks to Captain Waterston instead of rendering first aid.

The court found that Captain Waterston, in firing on the said PWI, acted properly in the execution of his military duty.[2]

A Dinner Party

That evening, following the Military Court of Inquiry, Captain Waterston, a lady friend, Captain Thomson and Major Archer, who was heading the army inquiry into the alleged mistreatment of prisoners at the Rowville camp, gathered in the officers' mess at the camp for a meal. Three Italian prisoners were on duty in the officers' mess and were waiting on the captain and his guests. They enjoyed a meal of meat, carrot and fish. The fish had been specially bought in Dandenong that day. They washed down their meal with six to eight bottles of beer.

Several months later, at Justice Simpson's inquiry into the alleged mistreatment of prisoners at Rowville, Thomson was asked about the events of the evening of the military inquiry. Thomson explained the events as follows.

'I sent Captain Waterston away on leave on Friday 5 April over the weekend. Captain Waterston came back to dinner at the camp with a lady friend. There was present at the time another major. The major had Captain Waterston's pistol – at this time it was necessary to permanently carry arms – you could not move around the camp unarmed. A silly bit of foolishness and larking occurred that night and a number of shots were fired by the Major and I fired one shot myself.'

'With Captain Waterston's pistol or revolver?'

The Military Court of Inquiry – Foolishness and Larking

'My pistol.'

'What were you armed with?'
'A .38 pistol and a .45.'

'Which one did you use?'
'The .45.'

'Where were the shots fired?'
'Into the roof.'

The commissioner and Thomson discussed for some time where the shots were fired, and the damage caused, which included a shattered lampshade and a light bulb from the light mounted on the ceiling. The commissioner continued his questioning of Thomson, asking how often he visited the camp.

'On the occasion when the party was held, was that an official visit?'
'It was not a party.'

'When the dinner party was held?'
'It was not a dinner party.'

'Well, when the shooting party was held?'
'It was not a shooting party.'

Rosario Schirinzi had been a witness at the Court of Inquiry that day. He was a friend of Rodolfo and had helped carry him to the infirmary on the night he was shot. Schirinzi was one of the prisoners on duty in the mess, waiting on the guests at the dinner after the inquiry. Schirinzi heard nine or ten shots fired in the officers' mess and saw the damaged light fittings, broken light bulb and bullet holes in the ceiling.

As we will read later, despite having just admitted that he fired the shots, Thomson later denied firing any shots in his court-martial hearing.

Vincenzo Renna, one of the Italian prisoners serving food, saw two guns on the table and heard joking and laughter as the shots were fired. He saw both Captain Thomson and Captain Waterston firing their pistols at the light.

Renna was asked, 'Was it a happy party?'
'Yes.'

At the time of the shooting, did you hear any voices from the party in the dining room?'
'I heard them joking amongst themselves.'[3]

New Camp Boundaries

On 10 April, after the Military Court of Inquiry and eleven days after the shooting, Captain Thomson placed a notice and map outside the orderly room with the camp boundary road marked in red. An English translation of the text was pasted over the Italian text when it was used as evidence in Justice Simpson's inquiry. Thomson instructed the camp leader to march all of the prisoners around the new camp boundary.

The outcome of the Military Court of Inquiry report was sent to Mr Forde, Minister for Army. He responded with the following memo which was marked 'Urgent':

> Death by shooting – PWI 48833, Bartoli, Rodolfo
>
> The report of the Court of Inquiry, forwarded by the Adjutant-General with his minute of 24 April 1946, is a most uninformative document and is the most unsatisfactory report of its nature that I can ever recollect having read.
>
> The court was called to report, among other things, on the circumstances under which this man sustained his injuries, including the cause of same; but the report as submitted is most indefinite and gives no real information as to the circumstance.

The Military Court of Inquiry – Foolishness and Larking

I assume that a full report of the Court of Inquiry will be made available to Mr Justice Simpson when he makes his investigation.[4]

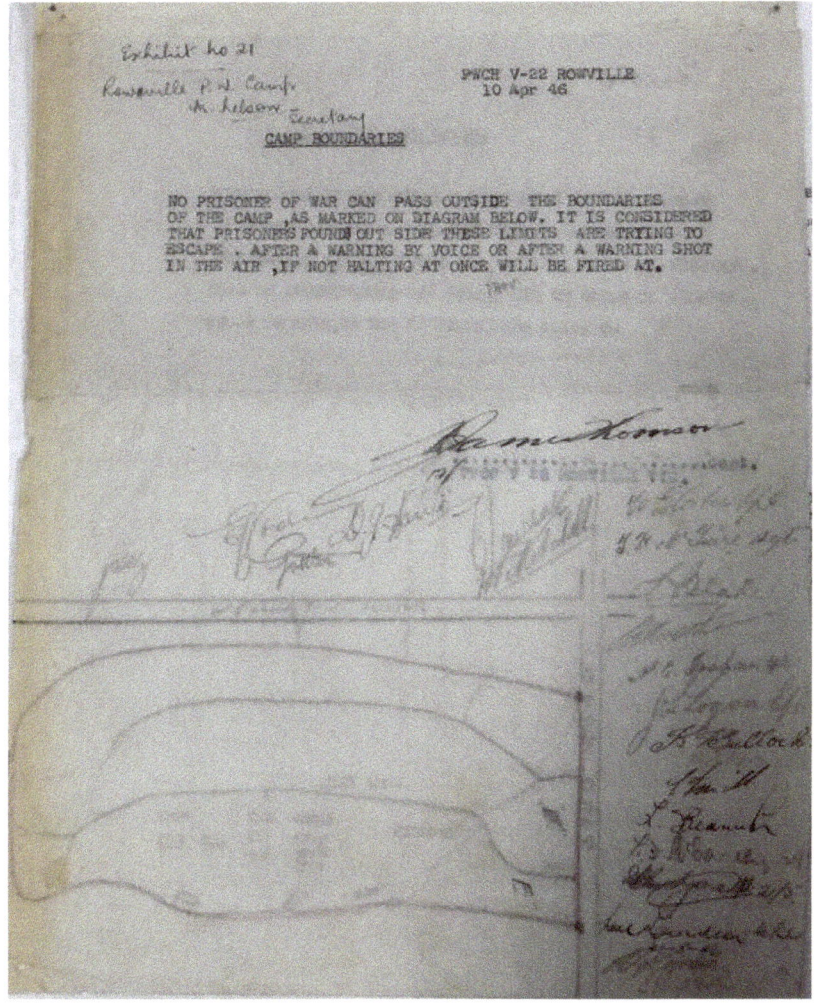

Captain Thomson's map, with new boundary in red[5]

CHAPTER 6

The Homicide Squad Investigates

DETECTIVE FREDERICK ADAM AND DETECTIVE CHARLES PETTY of the Homicide Squad in Melbourne were instructed to investigate the circumstances of the death of Rodolfo Bartoli for the Coroner. They made initial inquiries on 5 April, interviewing Dr Wales from the Heidelberg Military Hospital and the Coroner's surgeon, Dr Wright-Smith, and they perused the reports at the morgue. Detective Adam had read in the newspaper that there was to be a Military Court of Inquiry on 5 April and sought and received permission from Colonel Christison, who was conducting the inquiry, to visit the camp on 9 April to continue their investigation.

Detectives Adam and Petty's investigation was separate to any other police inquiries undertaken so far. Detective Howard from Dandenong Police Station visited the camp the day after the shooting, but no further action was taken. The call from Captain Waterston and the visit from the D24 wireless patrol and provost on the evening of the shooting was only to assist with any disturbance in the camp as a result of the shooting. At that stage, there hadn't been a death and the police considered the circumstances around the shooting to be a military matter.

Captain Waterston gave a statement about the events of the day and the circumstances of the shooting to Detective Petty. This statement was later used in the Coroner's Inquest and Justice Simpson's inquiry.

John Walker Waterston states:
I am a Captain of the Australian Military Forces and Prisoner of War Control Officer, V.22 Prisoner of War Hostel, Rowville.

I have been Commandant of V.22 Prisoner of War Hostel, Rowville since 18 February 1945. The hostel was set up for the purpose of employing Prisoner of War Italians on military works such as the salvage depot, Fishermen's Bend, engineer's depot Oakleigh and military camp Watsonia.

Later it was decided to use the hostel as a transit camp in addition to employment projects and it was being used for these purposes on 30 March 1946.

The hostel was originally a military camp. There is no fence built for the purpose of confining prisoners in the camp.

About nine months ago, I appointed Brigadier Scuma, an Italian prisoner of war, as camp leader. On his appointment, I advised him of the camp boundaries and indicated to him sketches of the area which were posted in the Prisoner of War Italian mess which is used by all Italian prisoners of war. It was his duty as camp leader to pass on all orders and instructions to prisoner of war Italians, including those in transit who are immediately handed over to him on arrival in the camp.

Every night at 6 pm, there is a parade of all prisoner of war Italians at the camp and they are counted and any new orders are passed on to them through the camp leader.

On 17 February 1946, eight Italian prisoners of war escaped from the camp and it was discovered that they were missing and I made a search of the surrounding district and I discovered two prisoners outside the camp area. I learned from them that their excuse for being outside the camp areas was that they could not read or write. After that date, on the next evening when the prisoners were lined up for counting, I caused the prisoners to be instructed verbally of the camp boundaries, and all instructions from that day onwards were given verbally to them. The deceased Bartoli was present at that time.

From time to time, there have been prisoners escape from the camp and on 30 March 1946 there were seventeen prisoners at large who had not been recaptured.

Luigi Melampo had escaped and had been recaptured and returned to the camp, and I sentenced him to twenty-eight days imprisonment to be served in Murchison, but he gave me an undertaking that he would not attempt to escape again if he was not imprisoned and I paroled him to myself and allowed him to remain at the camp. I am always of the belief that the prisoners were assisted in their escape by persons not connected with the camp because the prisoners quite frequently took their cases and gear with them. I was suspicious that they used to be picked up in cars in Stud Road south of the camp where there is a depression in the road.

On 30 March 1946 during the afternoon, I noticed two prisoners removing bread and jam from the PWI storeroom but they disappeared before I could intercept or get near them. Later that afternoon, I caught two prisoners named S Viviani No.46920 and A Guglielmetti No.48522 with a bag of lettuce which had been taken from the engineer's garden at the main gate of the camp. I questioned them but could not gain any information from them.

On account of seeing two prisoners with bread and jam and finding these two prisoners with lettuces and the suspicious activity of other prisoners, I formed the opinion that they were planning an escape that night. I also believed that on previous occasions the prisoners had escaped shortly after the 6 pm count and that would give them four and a half hours before the next count at 10.30 pm. I had the experience only a week previously of a stabbing between two prisoners at the property of a district resident at 7 pm although both prisoners had been present at the 6 pm count.

On this evening I placed two guards in Stud Road to watch for prisoners escaping and any suspicious cars. Sergeant Major McDougall and I proceeded to the south side of the camp and we parted and patrolled that area. Sergeant Major McDougall had a pistol and I a .303 rifle. At about 7 pm, I was south-east of the camp boundary, about 150 yards outside it, and I saw a prisoner which later turned out to be Bartoli. He was standing on the camp side of the road. He stood there for a while and was looking in all directions as if ascertaining if he was being observed. He suddenly crossed the road and started to run towards the fence and running at an angle which meant if he took a straight course would have passed about thirty yards from me.

I called out 'Stop!' and, without looking towards me, he altered his course and turned, going south-west. I fired a shot well into the air over his head and I ran along parallel with the fence and I could see that he was making for the scrub and I fired in the direction of his feet level and about a yard in front of him. When I fired, the prisoner fell. I ran up to him, not thinking that he had been shot and discovered that he had been.

I met Sergeant Major McDougall coming towards the spot and dispatched him immediately for the PWI doctor and stretcher bearers.

I had noticed when the prisoner was running through the scrub that he had something bulky under his burgundy tunic, but after he had been shot, I became excited and forgot to look at what it was.

As soon as Sergeant Major McDougall had gone for the doctor and the stretcher bearers, I went to the orderly room and telephoned for an ambulance from Heidelberg. PWI Galli shortly afterwards informed me that the prisoner was badly hurt and should be got to hospital immediately. I ordered my own staff car and dispatched the deceased to Heidelberg Military Hospital in it. Dr Galli and Brigadier Scuma went with him to hospital. I would estimate that it was easily twenty yards south of the road where the prisoner fell.

After the shooting, Dr Galli and Brigadier Scuma came to the orderly room door and Galli said, 'The camp is two hundred strong and we are all armed with knives and we are going to deal with you all tonight.' I called the civil police who came, and the prisoners were ordered to bed and lights put out.

Some months ago, I was asleep in my quarters when I was awakened by the noise of someone trying to get the door open and on investigating, I saw about six prisoners disappearing into the darkness. I discovered the time was 3 am.

I always carry arms at night time which are concealed but I never carry any in the day time.

When I fired the shot that struck the deceased, I did not intend to hit him. I only wanted to stop him, and I made sure that I only fired at ground level.

Bartoli had been through this camp on different occasions and had been on a farm in Koo Wee Rup and had refused duty and had been sentenced to twenty-eight days by Captain Drake on 9 October 1945 and was returned to my camp on transit to Murchison to serve his sentence and, on reaching my camp, I released him from detention on parole on my own account.

On 16 October 1945, I transferred him to Balcombe and on 21 December 1945 he was returned to me on account of his misbehaviour. On 10 January 1946, I gave him another chance and employed him on the 24th Maintenance Platoon and he was at that employment almost to the time of his death.

On return of the prisoners from various farms and centres, on army instructions I confiscated all civilian articles of clothing possessed by them which I forwarded to the Murchison Prisoner of War Holding Company and it is my belief that all clothing is forwarded to UNRRA [the United Nations Relief and Rehabilitation Administration].

On 30 March 1946, I was in Dandenong from about 11 am when I left the camp and returned at 1 pm and while in Dandenong I had two or three glasses of beer and I did not have any after that; in fact, there is no canteen in the camp.

signed
JW Waterston Capt.
(statement taken by CH Petty, Detective, 9.4.46)[1]

The camp diary corroborates Waterston's statement about a knife fight. There is an entry for 22 March about a knife fight between prisoners. One was arrested, and one sent to hospital. The captain went to Dandenong Police Station the following day as part of the investigation into the 'affray'.[2]

After taking Waterston's statement, Detective Petty asked him where the discharged cartridges had gone after the two shots had been fired. Waterston said that he didn't know, that he was aware of some in the office and that the cartridges may be among those.

Detective Petty was asked later at Justice Simpson's inquiry about the differences in Waterston's account of events that night from the brief statement given to the wireless patrol. The short statement from the night of the shooting had mentioned a prisoner crawling under the wire and implied that only one shot had been fired. Detective Petty said that he hadn't spoken to the constables who had attended on the night of the shooting as he understood they were only there to quell a disturbance and that their visit was nothing to do with the shooting.

On their visit to the camp the following day, 10 April, the detectives were accompanied by Mr Petzer of the Swiss Consul of the protecting power for the prisoners of war. At 4 pm with camp interpreter Sergeant Adamsohn, they paraded the prisoners. Detective Adam announced to the prisoners, 'We are detectives from Melbourne. We are making inquiries into the shooting of Rodolfo Bartoli for the Coroner who is going to hold an inquest. If anyone knows anything of the shooting of Bartoli, step forward.' Nine prisoners stepped forward.

Detective Petty asked, 'Does anyone know why Bartoli was shot?' No one stepped forward. The detective asked, 'Can anyone say what Bartoli was doing south of the road when he was shot?' No one stepped forward.

During their visit to the camp, the detectives were taken to the south road of the camp near the latrine where the shooting took place. At Justice Simpson's inquiry, Detective Adam described what he saw there. 'I saw a blood-stained handkerchief below the south of the road. There was some blood on the gravel and grass there. We took some samples of that and later on, on the 12th, I made certain measurements in that locality.'

The prisoner tents, latrine and south boundary road with Detective Adam (foreground) and camp interpreter Sergeant Adamsohn (background)

Detective Adam explained the scene shown in the photograph. 'I am standing where the bloodstains and the handkerchief were. The distance from there to a concrete drain is 31 feet to the edge. It is 75 feet to the middle of the roadway and 105 in a direct line to the lavatory or latrine.'

Captain Waterston had originally taken the detectives to where he thought the shooting had taken place, a location nearer the boundary fence, a little over 300 feet from where the photo was taken. However, the only place where bloodstains were found is the location shown in the photograph.

When asked about the camp boundaries, Waterston explained to the detectives that the wire fence was the camp boundary and that after 1800 hours the southern road became the boundary. Anyone found below the latrines after this hour would be considered out of bounds. Along with the number of shots allegedly fired, the topic of the definition of camp boundaries becomes a key issue in the Coroner's Inquiry and Justice Simpson's inquiry soon to follow.[3 4]

CHAPTER 7

Major Archer's Report – No Grounds for Complaint

MAJOR ARCHER'S REPORT WAS COMPLETED ON 9 APRIL. The scope of Major Archer's investigation was the allegations made in Mrs Santospirito's letter. Since the letter didn't detail any specific prisoners' names or times of the alleged acts, the Major decided to spend several days at the Rowville camp to 'obtain an accurate estimation of the administration'. Major Archer's inspection of the camp coincided with the Military Court of Inquiry and the 'mess dinner party' which he attended. While on site, he interviewed three of the staff: Captain Waterston, Captain Thomson and Sergeant Major McDougall. He also interviewed two Italian prisoners: Dr Trucco who had arrived one week earlier to replace Dr Galli as the camp doctor, and Enrico Veronelli who was an orderly in the camp hospital.

In the summary of Major Archer's report, he states that he checked the meal rations and found them to be satisfactory. A copy of the camp rations stocktake sheet shows an adequate quantity of food supplied, including the addition of spaghetti and macaroni. He examined the clothing allowance and other entitlements. The prisoners were found to have the clothing that they were entitled to, with the exception of some army boots which appeared to have been stolen from the salvage depot at Fishermen's Bend. He examined the medical records and found no record of a POW being sent to hospital and requiring seven stitches. There was no evidence of Jews or a reference about Captain Waterston being a protected person.

Major Archer put a series of questions about the allegations to each of the soldiers. Captain Waterston said that he often rode in a mail truck to Dandenong on a weekday to do some shopping and visit a hotel but had never been in an intoxicated condition while on duty. He would carry a concealed firearm when on patrol but said, 'I am at a loss to answer the allegation that I brandish a pistol in mid-air. Such an allegation is without foundation. Regarding physical violence, my answer is a complete denial of the allegation.' The captain was asked about the daily diet of bread and water and he explained that this punishment was only awarded for an offence committed by a prisoner while under detention and that it could not be awarded without confirmation from a higher authority. When questioned about confiscating clothing and items from prisoners, the captain explained that stolen items, civilian clothing which could be used as a disguise or items which could be used as weapons were confiscated.

Major Thomson, Waterston's superior officer, gave similar answers to the questions put to him and commended Captain Waterston on his character and his ability to carry out his duties effectively. He explained that Rowville was a difficult camp to manage and when talking about the prisoners said, 'These prisoners include some of the worst types charged with varying offences under the Crimes Offences Act. Captain Waterston has handled many delicate situations in the Rowville camp caused, in some instances, by PWI who would do anything rather than return to a compound at Murchison where they fear retaliation at the hands of their countrymen. This fear, aided and abetted by local residents who cunningly harboured prisoners from the Rowville Camp, was in many ways responsible for the escapes from the Rowville Camp.'

Both the Italian prisoners and medical personnel interviewed, Trucco and Veronelli, were asked a very small number of questions about the quality of the food, the treatment of prisoners and the medical history of two prisoners. There was no record of a prisoner receiving seven stitches in his forehead. Trucco explained in his statement that he could only provide information on the conditions to the best of his knowledge and could not state what conditions were like before his arrival. The report didn't include the fact that he had only been at the Rowville camp for one week and, despite being qualified as a dentist and not a doctor, had been moved to Rowville to replace Doctor Galli.[1]

On 18 April 1946, Major Archer's report into his investigations at the Rowville camp was sent to Mr Sinclair, the Secretary to the Minister for Army, with the following covering note:

Ref your minute 21 Mar 46

It is desired to forward herewith report of the officer appointed to investigate the allegations against Capt Waterston referred to in your minute under reference.

It is observed that the investigating officer has found no evidence to support the charges of habitual drunkenness and ill treatment of PW [sic] made against Capt Waterston, or the statement that food supplied to PW is very scanty. Articles confiscated from PW were found by the investigating officer to be only those items improperly in their possession and his report concludes that no legitimate grounds for complaint exist.[2]

Major Archer cleared Captain Waterston and the camp administration of any wrongdoing. However, his presence at the dinner party on the night of the Military Court of Inquiry calls into question the independence and integrity of his investigation. Fortunately, other formal inquiries were already proceeding.

CHAPTER 8

The Coroner's Inquest – the Shooting of Rodolfo

THE CORONER'S INQUEST INTO THE DEATH OF RODOLFO Bartoli commenced on 15 May 1946. Twenty-seven witnesses were heard. Fourteen Italian prisoners and six military personnel who were present at the camp on the night of the shooting appeared. Also present were three medical staff from the hospital and the Coroner's office, a medical chemist who analysed blood samples taken from the scene of the shooting, as well as two homicide detectives and a local farmer. None of the police from the Wireless Patrol who attended on the night of the shooting were requested to appear. The inquest ran for three days and was heard by Coroner JW Warwick with Mr AJ Aird assisting the Coroner. Mr Adami appeared on behalf of the Swiss Consul, the protecting power for Italian interests and Mr Maurice Goldberg represented Captain Waterston.

Captain Waterston and the military personnel who were present at the Military Court of Inquiry gave a similar account of events on the night of the shooting at this inquest. With new witness statements from some of the other military personnel present on the night and new statements from some of the prisoners, we begin to get a different perspective of events on the night of the shooting and a sense that Captain Waterston's account of events might not have been accurate.

The original transcript and copies of the Coroner's Inquest transcript are held by the National Archives and the Public Record Office Victoria. These transcripts only include one side of the courtroom conversation, the witness statements and responses to questions.

WITNESSES in the inquest resumed today at the Coroner's Court into the shooting of an Italian P.O.W. at Rowville prison camp on March 30. From left: Capt. J. Waterston, the Camp Commandant; Michelle Schuma, camp leader; two Italian P.O.W. witnesses, and former Warrant Officer H. McDougall.

The Herald, Thursday 16 May 1946[1]

Rodolfo was twenty-six years old when he died. His military record shows that he was from Florence and, prior to the war, had been employed as a civil servant. He was a private in the Italian Infantry and was captured in Libya on 10 December 1940. Rodolfo arrived in Sydney aboard the Queen Elizabeth on 15 October 1941 and was interned at the POW camp in Cowra, New South Wales. In August 1944, he was relocated to Murchison in Victoria and then to Rowville in December 1944 where, according to his service and casualty form, he spent most of his time.[2] He was sent to the Koo Wee Rup camp for one week in early October 1945 and then to the Balcombe camp, Mount Martha, on 16 October. He returned to Rowville on 21 December 1945.[3]

The Coroner's Inquest – the Shooting of Rodolfo

Rodolfo was 5 ft 10 inches tall (178 centimetres). He was well liked by prisoners and staff in the camp. Rodolfo was employed in the camp quartermaster store where prisoners could request uniforms or supplies when required. It was common knowledge among the long-term prisoners and the Australian personnel that Rodolfo had met a young woman on a nearby farm owned by the Gearon family. A small number of the prisoners were aware that Rodolfo had a bicycle hidden in some scrub by the bank of the Dandenong Creek just south of the camp and, on occasion, he used to leave the camp on his bike. Sergeant Major McDougall was asked about Rodolfo during Justice Simpson's inquiry, which occurred several months later, and commented that he was aware that Rodolfo had a girl in the district, and that he hoped to settle down and marry. Mr Minogue who represented Waterston at Justice Simpson's inquiry, told the inquiry that he had in his possession a letter from Rodolfo to Mr Gearon's daughter 'which refers in very affectionate terms to his daughter'. A number of prisoners remarked throughout the inquiry that the Gearon farm was a place where prisoners were welcome and a number of them would regularly visit the farm.[4]

Rodolfo Bartoli (back row, third from the right) at Cowra in 1944

At the Coroner's Inquest, Dr Wales, who performed surgery on Rodolfo, described to the courtroom Rodolfo's injuries and the medical treatment that had been provided to try to save his life. Despite the treatment, Rodolfo died at 23.30 on the evening of the shooting. Dr Wales was of the opinion that the cause of death was a gunshot wound and that, due to the extent of Rodolfo's injuries, it was unlikely that he would have survived, even if he had received immediate hospital care. During the Coroner's Inquest, Doctor Mollison read the notes made by Dr Wright-Smith who performed the autopsy, as Dr Wright-Smith had unfortunately passed away since performing the autopsy. The autopsy found that Rodolfo was generally in good health and there was evidence of surgery having taken place to treat his wounds. Dr Wright-Smith's findings reinforced those of Dr Wales, stating that Rodolfo's injuries were so serious that they would have been fatal, regardless of the treatment he received.

Waterston's statement, which had been taken by the homicide detectives on 9 April 1946, was read out in the Coroner's Inquest by Detective Sergeant Petty. During the inquest, Waterston responded to questions about the events around the shooting. His account was mostly the same as the one provided to the police, but in this version, he added that he recalled that the prisoner was carrying something bulky under his tunic. However, after the prisoner had been shot, he forgot to check what the prisoner had been carrying as his main concern was getting the prisoner medical attention.

Waterston was also questioned further about the missing spent cartridges from his rifle and it was pressed upon him that, given the dispute around the definition of the camp boundaries and the number of shots fired, this was important evidence. Waterston said that he had been unable to find the cartridges. Waterston also states that he had difficulty in understanding the angle of the bullet entry and exit as it did not seem possible, based on his evidence of where he was standing and where Bartoli was standing at the time the shot was fired. 'He was on my right. He would be moving more or less towards my front left, as I judged it then. I heard evidence that the bullet entered into the right groin and I heard its course as described. As to accounting for how the bullet took that course, I cannot; at the angle he was to me at the time, unless he had turned again...His right side was not towards me when I fired, he was more or less frontal. The way I have described it, I should have thought that the bullet would have entered more on his left side than his right.'[5]

Putting together the statements of witnesses who were in the vicinity of the shooting and who gave evidence at the Coroner's Inquest and Justice Simpson's inquiry a few weeks later, a timeline of events becomes clearer.

On Saturday 30 March, after spending several hours in Dandenong visiting the police station, doing some shopping and having two or three glasses of beer at a hotel, Waterston returned to the camp at 1 pm. At about 4.30 pm, Waterston caught two prisoners, Guglielmetti and Viviani, in the engineer's garden taking lettuces. He and Sergeant McDougall questioned them, searched their rooms, found their bags open and sitting on their beds and came to the conclusion that the prisoners had been planning an escape. They were then locked in the guardhouse.

At around 6 pm, the captain entered the orderly room where several soldiers and drivers were playing cards. Waterston seemed agitated and looked flushed. He told the soldiers to be alert and said that he suspected trouble. Waterston instructed Corporals McCarthy and Logan to arm themselves and patrol Stud Road to look for possible escapees. If one was found, they were instructed to hold the prisoner and to fire a shot in the air to get the captain's attention. The remaining soldiers stayed in the orderly room and continued their card game. According to Corporal McCarthy, nothing unusual had happened in the camp that day or evening; everything seemed normal.

Waterston went to his office and took a .303 rifle which was leaning against the wall in the corner behind his office door while Sergeant Major McDougall armed himself with a .38 pistol. The two soldiers headed down the hill to the southern boundary of the camp to begin their patrol.

The evening mess rollcall had been completed and all prisoners were present. The prisoners were having their evening meal, consisting of a soup and a main course, both of which were brought to the prisoners' tables by prisoners on mess duty. Due to the number of prisoners in the camp, the evening meal was held in two shifts. Bartoli ate during the first meal shift that evening.

After finishing his meal, Bartoli spoke to a fellow prisoner, Mattia Natale, outside the mess hut. Natale told Bartoli that he was going for a walk. Bartoli said to him, 'I am going down here to the latrines and, if you will wait for a while, we will go together.' Natale replied, 'In case you come back, I will wait for you near the mess.'[6]

Bartoli and camp leader Michele Scuma began walking down the hill together towards the southern road and toilet block. They were discussing a card game that Bartoli had lost earlier that day and Scuma was teasing him about it. Bartoli had said to Scuma, 'Next time it will be my luck.'[7]

It had been an overcast day. The sun was setting but the light was still good enough to see people at quite a distance. About thirty metres before the toilet block, Bartoli and Scuma parted company. As Bartoli was walking past the nearby tents, Francisco Pellicano called out, 'Foffo, where are you going?' Bartoli replied, 'I am going to the toilet.' Scuma had gone into the toilet but Bartoli continued walking past the toilet block and headed over the road.[8]

About a minute later, a loud shot was heard. Adamo Marsi and Carmelo Perugini, who were both at their tents nearby, heard the shot. Marsi saw Bartoli fall to the ground. Five other prisoners, also at their tents, saw Bartoli on the ground immediately after he had been shot. Bartoli was lying on his left side and tried to get up but was unable to. He turned to them and called out 'Aiuto' (Help). Several of the prisoners saw Waterston, carrying his rifle, walk up to Bartoli, bend down, touch Bartoli and then walk towards the office. Three of the prisoners – Marsi, Perugini and Pellicano – saw Waterston walking from the south-west, the opposite direction to Waterston's evidence. Immediately after the sound of the shot, Perugini saw Waterston about thirty metres from Bartoli, holding his rifle horizontally and then sling it over his shoulder.[9]

Scuma rushed out of the toilet and saw a group of men at the tents looking around. Before the war, Scuma had been a policeman in Italy and was used to dealing with situations of crisis. He asked the approaching prisoners to stay where they were while he assessed the situation. He saw Waterston walking away towards his office. Scuma walked down to Bartoli. Bartoli said, 'They shot me, I don't know why.' Scuma asked, 'Who has killed you?' Bartoli replied, 'I do not know.'[10,11]

Sergeant Major McDougall said that he had heard shouts of warning and two shots and rushed to Waterston's location. Waterston told McDougall, 'A prisoner has been shot. Go up and get the doctor and stretcher bearers.' McDougall didn't approach Bartoli; he ran directly to the hospital and then went back to the office. Both Dr Galli and McDougall mention a comment made by Dr Galli. He told McDougall that the camp was two hundred strong and that Waterston was here alone. Galli told the inquiry that he said this because he was concerned that, with the prisoners being upset, someone might have done something stupid. However, McDougall took it as a threat. McDougall's version of the comment was that 'The camp is two hundred strong and we are all armed with knives and we are going to deal with you tonight.'[12]

About five minutes later, some prisoners arrived with a stretcher to take Bartoli to the camp hospital. The prisoners put Bartoli onto the stretcher. Schirinzi recalls seeing Bartoli earlier in the evening eating in the mess hut. Schirinzi helped to carry Bartoli to the camp hospital and to undress him for the doctor. Aldo Poggi, a good friend of Bartoli, had heard the shot from the mess hall. A few minutes later, Poggi was washing his plates near his tent when he heard prisoners running around saying that a prisoner had been shot. Poggi saw Waterston walk past with a rifle in his hand and then Bartoli being carried on a stretcher with his arms hanging over the side. Poggi called out to him, Bartoli answered. Poggi rushed over to help carry the stretcher.[13]

Galli did what he could to minimise Bartoli's wound. Bartoli asked Galli, 'Am I serious, doctor?' Galli tried to reassure him and told him it wasn't serious. Galli reported that Bartoli was saying to himself, 'He has killed me, he has killed me.' The camp padre, Joseph Raimondi, also tried to console Bartoli and keep him calm by providing him with 'religious comforts'. Poggi stayed by Bartoli's side. Bartoli was crying and saying, 'They have killed me, they have killed me.' Poggi asked him, 'But did you see the captain shoot you?' Bartoli replied, 'No, I have seen nobody. I only heard the shot and found myself on the ground.' Bartoli had been wearing his burgundy prisoner uniform, and none of the prisoners who assisted treating him and undressing him saw any sign that he had being carrying anything or attempting to conceal anything under his clothing.

After assessing Bartoli, Dr Galli went to Waterston's office and Waterston informed him that an ambulance had been called. When Galli returned to his patient, he could see that Bartoli was in a grave situation and asked Scuma to go to the captain to arrange a car to take him to hospital, instead of waiting for an ambulance. A car and driver arrived and Bartoli was rushed to the Heidelberg Military Hospital. Galli, Scuma and Poggi travelled in the car with Bartoli.

The following morning at the request of Captain Thomson, camp leader Scuma and camp doctor Galli were asked to pack up their belongings and were relocated to Puckapunyal. Padre Raimondi was also removed from the camp as part of a separate and unrelated arrangement.

During the Coroner's Inquest, allegations began to emerge about Waterston regularly drinking alcohol and being under the influence of alcohol at the time of the shooting. Galli was of the opinion that he was acting differently, either due to excitement or due to drinking. Waterston refuted Galli's suggestion that he had been drinking. 'As to Dr Galli saying he considered me agitated and under the influence, he was not in any position to judge anybody's sobriety: he was running round like a hysterical schoolgirl, and so was Scuma.'[14]

All the witnesses questioned at the inquiry who were present that night, except for Waterston and McDougall, only heard one shot and did not hear any verbal warning prior to the shot. There were clear instructions about under which circumstances an Australian soldier was allowed to fire upon a prisoner. These were outlined in the Routine Army Orders issued in September 1943. They state: 'A prisoner of war endeavouring to escape could be fired upon, but a warning, if possible, should be given first.'

Thomson and Waterston said in their evidence that the camp boundaries had been altered since the escape of eight prisoners on 18 February and that the prisoners had been notified through the camp leader, Scuma. The Geneva Convention requires that prisoners be notified of any changes to the camp boundaries. The notice must be posted in the prisoners' mess in the native language of the prisoners. This didn't happen until 10 April, eleven days after the shooting. Throughout the Coroner's Inquest, the prisoners questioned about the camp boundaries said that they were aware of a change but, as far as they knew, the change just meant that they weren't allowed on the main roads in Rowville after the 6 pm mess call. Apart from that limitation, they were free to roam the camp until lights out.

The military personnel stationed at Rowville weren't aware of the limits of the camp boundaries. McDougall, who says that he was in charge of all camp administration, didn't put up any notices about a change in boundaries, nor had he instructed anyone to do so. He was aware that there was a copy of the Geneva Convention in the camp but did not know where it was and didn't have a copy of it himself. When questioned if he knew about the requirement of posting notices in the mess about changes in boundaries, he responded, 'As to knowing if there is such a rule, I could not say.'[15]

Both prisoners and military personnel acknowledged that there was little to prevent a prisoner from trying to escape and that the fence surrounding the camp was a simple wire farm fence.

After hearing three days of evidence, the Coroner concluded with the following statement in his report:

> Having inquired upon the part of our Lord the King when, where, and how and by what means the said Rodolfo Bartoli came by his death, I say that on the 30th day of March, 1946 at No.115 General Hospital, Heidelberg, in the said state, the said Rodolfo Bartoli died from the effects of a gunshot wound of the abdomen, inflicted on him by John Walker Waterston, at Rowville Prisoner of War Camp, on 30 March 1946, but from the evidence adduced, I am unable to say whether the killing was justifiable or otherwise.[16]

The Coroner's Inquest – the Shooting of Rodolfo

The Truth, 25 May 1946[17]

Several weeks before the shooting, Scuma had written a letter of complaint to the Swiss Consulate, the Red Cross and Murchison Headquarters, describing the events around the shooting. He stated that he, Doctor Galli and another prisoner had heard Captain Waterston saying that he intended to kill a prisoner. When Doctor Galli objected, he was told that he too would be put out of the way if he tried to interfere.[18]

On the evening before the Coroner's Inquest, 14 May, as the prisoners were arriving back at the camp by truck after their day of working, Captain Waterston approached one of the trucks. He singled out a prisoner seated in the back of one of the trucks, Enrico Quintavalle. Waterston slapped Quintavalle in the face and told him to get off the truck. He took Quintavalle into the office with Sergeant Holtham, a camp interpreter. Waterston continued to slap Quintavalle's face as he questioned him about a conversation that he had heard that Quintavalle had had with Mr Gearon and two other men. The subject of the conversation had been a rumour that the captain had shot Bartoli because Bartoli knew too much about a large quantity of corrugated iron from a dismantled camp hut being delivered to Mr Finn's farm, the farm where Quintavalle was employed.

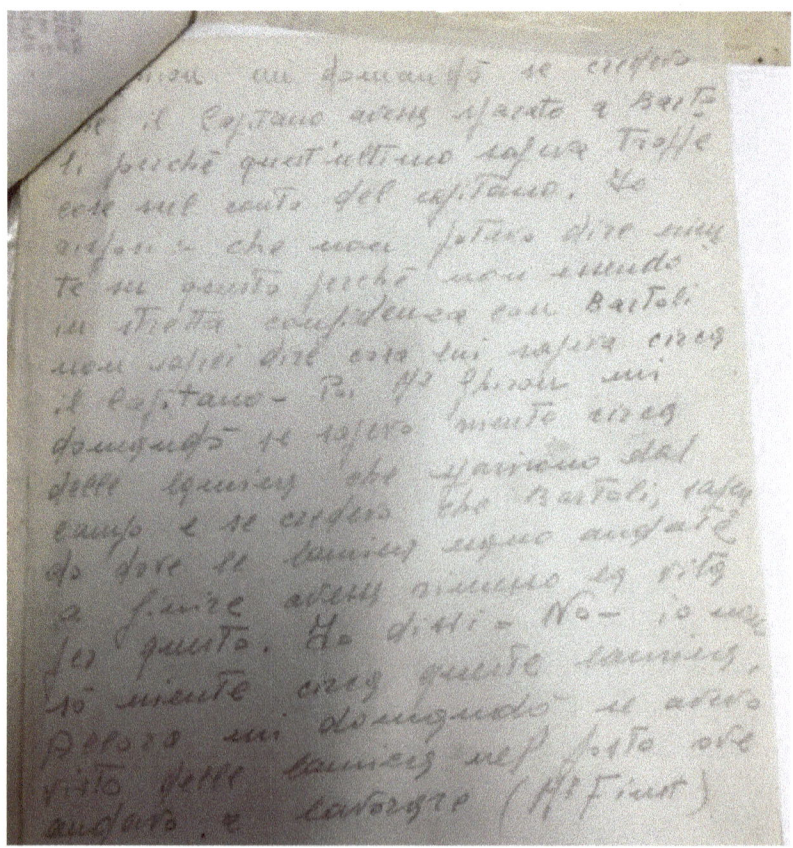

The Coroner's Inquest – the Shooting of Rodolfo

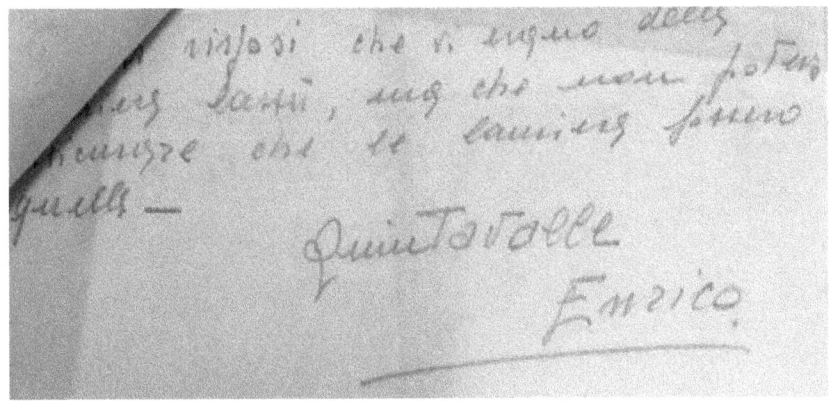

Enrico Quintavalle's handwritten statement in Italian

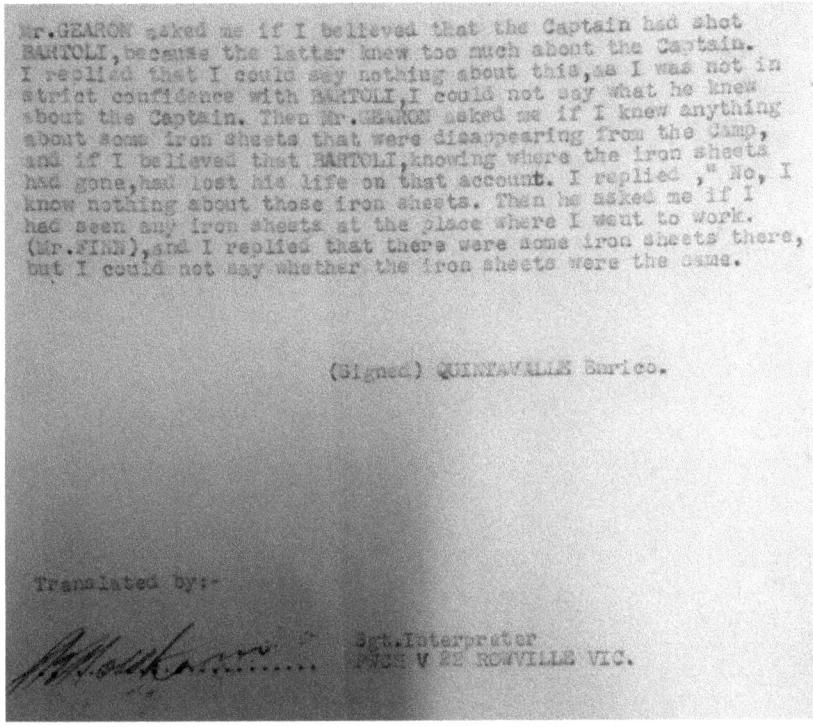

English translation of Enrico Quintavalle's statement[19]

CHAPTER 9

A Veritable Nero – Justice Simpson's Inquiry Commences

Justice Simpson's inquiry commenced on 28 May. The allegations contained in Mrs Santospirito's letter were used to form the terms of reference for the inquiry. Justice Simpson used the following questions during the inquiry to address the terms of reference.

- Did Captain Waterston assault prisoners of war or use physical force in relation to them?

- Was Captain Waterston on any occasion under the influence of drink while on duty in the camp, and if so, to what extent?

- Did Captain Waterston improperly take from any prisoner of war any articles of value belonging to the said prisoner of war?

- Did Captain Waterston brandish or fire a revolver in or near the vicinity of the camp?

- Was the food in the camp ample in quantity and of good quality?

- Was Captain Waterston's conduct connived at by his superiors or by any of them?

In addition to these questions, the inquiry was asked to investigate the circumstances resulting in the death of the Italian POW, Rodolfo Bartoli, and whether the administration of the Rowville POW Control Hostel was satisfactory or otherwise, and the measures which should be taken to address any issues identified.[1]

Throughout the inquiry, Justice Simpson was assisted by Mr CA Sweeney. Mr JF Moloney was instructed by Mr VR Adami and appeared for the Swiss Consul, the protector for Italian interests. The Department of Army was represented by Colonel JF Flannagan and later in the proceedings, Mr J Minogue represented Captain Waterston.

At the beginning of the inquiry, questions were asked about the source of the information included in Mrs Santospirito's letter. Legal officer in the Deputy Commonwealth Crown Solicitor's Office, Gerald Healy, had been given the task to make inquiries about the letter. He interviewed Mrs Santospirito who said that, while she had written the letter, she did not have firsthand knowledge of the issues in the camp. She had been given the information from Mrs Ganora of Mordialloc who had received the information from Mrs Siletta and Mrs Biletta of Warrigul Road, Oakleigh. Mrs Biletta was a cousin of one of the prisoners, Aldo Poggi, who was a personal friend of Rodolfo. Poggi said later in the inquiry that he had written to his cousin a number of times. The Commissioner decided that it was clear that the author of the letter would not be able to give evidence and Mr Sweeney agreed that it would be idle to call someone who had information that was, at best, third hand.[2]

The inquiry sat for a total of nineteen days between 28 May and 16 August 1946. One hundred and six witnesses were heard, with Justice Simpson's final report being delivered on 26 August 1946.

At the time of Justice Simpson's inquiry, Captain John Walker Waterston was thirty-four years old. He was 6 ft 1 inch tall with a solid build. Waterston enlisted in the army in October 1939 as a Private and

A Veritable Nero – Justice Simpson's Inquiry Commences

was posted to the 2nd/6th Battalion. After receiving training at Seymour, he was commissioned in June 1940 and spent some time in Australia before being shipped to Palestine. During his time overseas, he served in Syria, Ceylon and New Guinea. He was promoted to the rank of Lieutenant in June 1940 and to Captain on 30 March 1943.

Waterston left New Guinea due to illness: malaria and dysentery. After some time in hospital, he was declared unfit for further tropical service and returned home in 1944. After a short period of leave, he was posted to the Prisoner of War Guard Battalion at Murchison and Graytown and was put in charge of the German compound. He was then moved to Colac. Waterston arrived at the Rowville camp on 30 January 1945 and took over as Camp Commandant on 18 February. He initially had seven staff reporting to him and was responsible for one hundred and fifty prisoners.

Captain Waterston[3 4]

In Waterston's opinion, the conditions in the camp were very poor when he arrived. Areas between the huts were overgrown with trees and prisoners had not been using the latrines and were fouling the areas around the huts. After several months of work, he improved the tidiness and the hygiene of the camp. He felt that discipline in the camp was poor. Prisoners would ignore lights out and the parade whistle, prisoners often taking twenty minutes to half an hour to assemble when called to parade. Camp boundaries were ignored, and prisoners were often found fraternising with civilians in the area. He found three stills around the camp used for making *bomba* or *grappa*. In one of the disused buildings, he found a bucket of prunes fermenting. Since part of the prisoners' dried fruit ration was being used to make grappa, the supply of dried fruit was stopped.[5]

A former prisoner, Phil Faella, who was interviewed as part of the Rowville Lysterfield History Project in 1996, also spoke about making *grappa* in the Rowville camp. 'The men made sure that the fruit scraps from the kitchen, such as banana peels and bruised grapes, were not thrown out but carefully put into clean bins which were then taken well away from the camp and hidden among the trees lining the bank of the Dandenong Creek. After a time, the fermented mash would be ready for distilling, which of course had to be done secretly. The men used to keep their bottles of *grappa* hidden on ledges at the top of the walls of the huts until one night when Captain Waterston found a bottle of the potent brew and confiscated it. He was known to enjoy a drink and didn't make a fuss about his discovery.'[6]

Throughout Justice Simpson's inquiry, there are numerous accounts of Captain Waterston inflicting what might be considered to be cruel and unnecessary treatment on prisoners. A few stand out. One is the assault in the lettuce patch on the night of the shooting where Waterston had decided that the theft of lettuces was an indication of an impending escape attempt that night.

Attilio Guglielmetti was in the Rowville camp from December 1944 through until April 1946. He, along with Viviani, was one of the prisoners that Waterston found in the engineer's garden on the afternoon that Bartoli was killed. Guglielmetti explained the incident.

'About half past four in the afternoon, I went out to get some lettuce from a garden bed in the vicinity of the gate at the Rowville camp.'

Mr Sweeney, assisting Justice Simpson at the inquiry, asked, 'How did you come to be getting the lettuce?'
'I just wanted to get some salad for ourselves.'

'Did you get the lettuce?'
'Yes.'

'What happened then?'
'Just as I picked a few heads of lettuce, Captain Waterston arrived from Dandenong. They took the truck into the camp and returned to the gate. The Captain walked up to us and hit me in the face.'

Guglielmetti explained that the captain hit him with an open hand on the left cheek. Mr Sweeney asked, 'Who gave the instruction to get the lettuce?'

Guglielmetti tried to explain that the Australian Sergeant, Sergeant Baggs, who was in charge of the squad that he was working for, had said that he could take some lettuce from the garden anytime that he wanted some.

'The other man got far more than I did. He got at least five or six similar hits, the same open-handed hits to the face,' Guglielmetti explained to Mr Sweeney.

'Was that the end of the incident?'
'Afterwards, he ordered an inspection of my belongings and took everything away from me and only left me in my underpants and singlet.'

The inspection took place in the open air, in the garden by the main gate. The captain took a silver matchbox from Guglielmetti. He told Guglielmetti to put his clothes back on but he didn't return the matchbox. Once he was dressed, the captain took Guglielmetti and Viviani back to their huts and searched their gear. He took some clothing and a small wallet from Guglielmetti. He then put Guglielmetti into the guardhouse for ten days without any explanation as to why he was in detention. Guglielmetti was never charged with an offence and his belongings were never returned. Viviani, who gives a similar account, had been in Rowville for about ten months. He was with Guglielmetti, collecting lettuces from the engineer's garden. Sweeney asked Viviani what happened after Captain Waterston arrived.

'He gave me a slap in the face and a kick in the buttock. He made me undress. He searched my gear and took away a watch. Then he gave me six slaps in the face and kicks in the back.'

'Where did Captain Waterston make you undress?'

A Veritable Nero – Justice Simpson's Inquiry Commences

'Where we were collecting the lettuce.'

With Viviani in just his underwear, Waterston took him to his hut and searched his things. Waterston took an alarm clock that Viviani had amongst his belongings. No official record was made of these items being taken and Viviani was not told why it was taken and was not given a receipt. Viviani and Guglielmetti were never told why they were being put into detention and, according to Viviani's recollection, they remained there for nine and a half days.

Viviani was asked what he had been instructed about the camp boundaries. He said that he had been told that they were allowed two miles down the main roads from the camp. He never saw a notice in the camp mess about the boundaries and often used to walk on the roads with other prisoners. He used to play football or soccer in the area south of the boundary road with other prisoners.[7]

One of the accounts of allegations of violence frequently inflicted by Captain Waterston presented during Justice Simpson's inquiry involved an unusual evening visit by two men dressed in dark suits.

At around 8 pm on 22 May 1945, two men arrived in a car at the camp. They drove up to the main gate and were met by Sergeant Heynemann, the camp interpreter. They were taken to Captain Waterston's office where they presented police badges and introduced themselves as Constable Leslie Harley and Constable Eric Haggis.

Constable Harley had just commenced leave and he and Constable Haggis were travelling from Sale to Melbourne to visit Constable Harley's mother. Once they had reached Dandenong, they stopped to have a meal at a café and decided to take a detour to Rowville. When asked why they decided to do that, Constable Harley replied, 'It was merely the fact that I was of the opinion that there were some German prisoners in Rowville at the time. I was in Germany in 1936 as a member of the last Olympic Games team, and I thought I may have seen somebody I knew. It was just idle curiosity.'[8]

They had a second meal for the evening with Captain Waterston in his office and were then taken on a tour of the camp. Sergeant Heynemann, the interpreter, accompanied them as they visited a number of the prisoners' huts and the messes.

At the inquiry, Captain Waterston and Constable Harley gave a matching account of a visit to the guardhouse which took place at the end of the tour of the camp. Heading back to the car, the captain mentioned that he needed to drive to Dandenong to pick up some prisoners and that the two constables could follow him since they were unfamiliar with the area. They followed the captain's car down the driveway. Before leaving the camp for Dandenong, the captain stopped his car just before the main gate and entered the guardhouse. The two policemen decided to follow him. They entered the guardhouse accompanied by Sergeant Heynemann. Five POWs were brought out of their cells, one by one, to collect blankets; they each picked up a blanket and went back into their cells. The policemen inspected some of the cells. In one of them, a prisoner was lying on the floor. The captain gave him a slap on his legs to make him get up. Apart from that incident, the visit was uneventful. Once the blankets were collected, the captain, the constables and the sergeant left the guardhouse and the constables followed the captain's car to Dandenong and continued their journey to Melbourne.

The five prisoners who were in the cells that night have a different recollection of events. According to the prisoners, the captain, Sergeant Heynemann and Constables Harley and Haggis opened the guardroom door and called each of the prisoners out one at a time to collect their blankets for the evening. As each prisoner walked through the door into the area where the soldiers and policemen were standing, they were either slapped or punched by Captain Waterston and one of the policemen. One of the prisoners was left with a bleeding nose, one an injured jaw that caused him difficulty in eating for two days and two with bleeding gums.

A Veritable Nero – Justice Simpson's Inquiry Commences

The reason for Captain Waterston and Constable Harley's similar version of events that evening became apparent during questioning at the inquiry when, to the astonishment of the courtroom, Constable Harley revealed that, after he had received his subpoena at 2 pm the day before he was to appear at the inquiry, he phoned the Rowville camp and asked for Captain Waterston. Captain Waterston sent a car to pick up Constable Harley and they spent the evening together at Captain Waterston's house, listening to a boxing match on the wireless. The match, which took place at Yankee Stadium, was rebroadcast on 3DB at 9 pm that evening and they would have heard Joe Louis knock out Billy Conn in the eighth round to retain his status as World Heavyweight Champion.[9] After the match, in Constable Harley's words, Waterston and Harley discussed the case. Constable Harley explained that they had discussed the details of the events of that night, where they went in the camp, and they agreed that no prisoners had been hit.

Despite the unusual circumstances of this visit and the fact that the two men got together on the evening before the inquest, Harley and Waterston claim they had never met before. Constable Harley had been an amateur heavyweight champion boxer for fifteen years and had represented Australia at the 1936 Olympic Games in Berlin. In 1947, he was dismissed from the police force. Harley was found guilty of an act of misconduct: assaulting a prisoner while in custody. He broke the prisoner's jaw in two places and left him unconscious in his cell.[10] Leslie Harley, no longer a police officer, was later employed as a civilian boxing and wrestling instructor at the Police Depot, then the Police Academy and at the Police Gym at Russell Street where he had a formidable reputation with both recruits and police officers. He retired from the role in 1976.

Harley was featured in an internal police magazine. The title of the article was 'Les Harley – human fighting machine'. A quote from the article says that, when he joined the academy as an instructor, 'with one hand he could open the window of an average sized room and simultaneously tear the door off the hinges with the other'.[11]

As well as the slaps, kicks and punches often inflicted upon prisoners, Waterston was accused of 'brandishing his pistol'. Two prisoners, Marchiafava and Pizzi, gave evidence at Justice Simpson's inquiry that Waterston had walked into the mess holding his pistol and fired a shot through the roof one evening when a group of men were sitting in the mess and refusing to go to work.[12]

When another prisoner, Cacciagrano, had arrived at the Rowville camp, he was taken into detention. He described the incident. 'It was about ten o'clock at night. Coming into the cell the captain gave two slaps in the face to another prisoner, Cagnese, and he fell to the ground. Then he came towards me and gave me a slap in the face. I took a step backwards and prepared to defend myself because I did not want to be hit again. He then pulled out the revolver and pointed it at me. Then he raised the revolver in the air and shot through the roof or upwards.'

Nesti, who was present in the cell, was of the opinion that Waterston was drunk when he slapped Cacciagrano. Nesti said, 'Cacciagrano became rebellious; he made a sign with his jacket and said "shoot".'

Mr Minogue asked the interpreter in the courtroom, 'Why did the witness point to his forehead?'

The interpreter replied, 'He says that the captain pointed the muzzle of the pistol at the forehead of Cacciagrano, then raised the pistol and fired it through the roof. The captain then took their blankets away and left them in the cells.'

Another incident which involved Nesti was over a dispute in the pay office. Nesti refused to sign for his pay because in the past he had signed paperwork and had never received the money. Waterston insisted that he sign. When Nesti refused, Waterston slapped him. Waterston walked into his office and returned holding a pistol. He fired two shots

A Veritable Nero – Justice Simpson's Inquiry Commences

towards the ground and then locked Nesti in the cells. Holtham, an Australian soldier and Italian interpreter, also witnessed the incident. Holtham explained to the captain what Nesti's objection was and Waterston said, 'He has got to sign, because whether he signs or not does not make a difference.' Nesti scrawled a mark which wasn't a signature, then Waterston poked him with his swagger stick and said, 'Get outside.' Cacciagrano was also told to sign but refused for the same reason. Waterston hit him across the face and Cacciagrano fought back. Waterston got one arm around Cacciagrano's head, holding him in a headlock and Sergeant Mathers took him by the feet and they carried him out of the office. The captain went back into his office, picked up his pistol and walked out and fired a couple of shots into the ground just by Cacciagrano's legs. Cacciagrano then pulled his shirt open and said in Italian, 'Shoot!' The captain ordered Cacciagrano and the other prisoners present into a truck to be taken to the detention cells.[13]

When asked about his swagger stick, Waterston replied, 'The stick I have is not exactly a swagger stick; it is a very light cane. The carpenter at the camp made it for me. As a matter of fact, he made me several. I usually break them by leaning on them. I use the stick, which is about 2 ft 6 inches long, for poking round odd places in the camp when on inspection, and quite frequently I have it in my hand when I am directing working parties or inspecting prisoners on the jobs in the camp. I have frequently shown prisoners what I wanted done, using the cane to indicate it.'

One evening in March 1946, Paolessi was standing near the mess hut when some prisoners had just returned from another centre. Paolessi recalls, 'I stood there watching, and I heard a pistol shot close to my feet. I turned around and saw the captain. He was standing about five or six metres away.' Waterston told Paolessi to go away, so Paolessi turned his back and walked away. Paolessi was asked what he meant by being shot close to his feet. He explained, 'Little stones were flying near my feet…the stones actually hit me.' He was of the opinion that the stones flying was caused by the bullet.[14]

One Saturday evening about two weeks before Bartoli was shot, Waterston ordered a late-night patrol of the camp between about 11 pm and 2 am. There had been a growing number of escapes and he said that he wanted to find out how the prisoners were escaping. At Justice Simpson's inquiry, Corporal Lee McCarthy recalled a night when he was on patrol on the south road of the camp and Waterston made the comment to him, with a smile on his face, 'I want to see a dead Eyetie tonight.' (Eyetie is a derogatory term, indicating an Italian person.) He didn't take it as a joke and thought that it was a serious comment. Holtham was present on patrol the same night and heard the same comment. Holtham also remembered the remark.[15]

Many witnesses were questioned about Waterston's drinking and responses were mixed. It seems clear that he was a regular drinker and he had admitted to having at least three drinks before returning to the camp on the day of the shooting. It is unclear whether he was impaired by alcohol when carrying out his duties. McKinnon was asked if he had seen the captain drunk. He said that twice he had seen him when he had appeared to have had a large amount of alcohol: one week prior to the shooting and the night of the shooting. The night of the shooting, he was very tense and angry. His face looked flushed.

Towards the end of the inquiry, Moloney put several questions to Waterston for which Waterston claimed privilege and was told by the commissioner that he did not have to answer if he felt that he may incriminate himself.

Moloney asked Waterston, 'Did you at any time promulgate any order in the camp that the camp boundaries as from shortly after 18 February were to be bounded by the road within the camp?'
Waterston replied, 'I do not think I should answer that question, Mr Moloney.'

A Veritable Nero – Justice Simpson's Inquiry Commences

The commissioner asked, 'Are you seeking to claim privilege on that question?'
'On that, I think so, sir.'

Mr Moloney continued, 'Did you ever, prior to any patrol say, "I want a dead Eyetie tonight"?'
Waterston replied, 'I think I would claim the same privilege on that question, if I may.'

The commissioner responded, 'All right, you do not need to answer it.'

Mr Moloney continued with his questions. 'On the night of 30 March, you were armed with a .303 rifle, were you not?'
'Concerning that shooting, sir, I would rather not answer any questions concerning that at all.'

'Do you mean you are claiming privilege not to answer anything in relation to the shooting?'
'Yes.'

Mr Moloney pressed on. 'Did you fire one shot or two shots?'
'I claim privilege for that question too.'[16]

Between the night of the shooting and the Coroner's Inquest, Captain Waterston had given four differing accounts of the shooting. He initially told the police who arrived to assist that he had seen a prisoner moving through the wire. He called on him to halt but he did not stop so he fired a shot. He didn't mention a warning shot.

Waterston provided an official statement to the army taken just after the shooting. This statement wasn't included as part of any of the inquiries or hearings but parts of it were used in a press release from the army on the following Monday.

> After spotting Bartoli, he explained, 'I again shouted loudly to him to halt, but he kept on towards the scrub. I attempted to catch him

and, on realising that he would beat me to the scrub, I fired a shot over his head. He continued to run for the scrub. I then fired a shot at his feet with the intention of kicking up dirt in front of him. The shot went high and the bullet struck him in the region of the groin.'[17]

There was the official statement given to the homicide detectives which was used as part of the Coroner's Inquest. Finally, Waterston also responded to questions at the Coroner's Inquest about the shooting and added the new detail about Bartoli carrying something bulky under his uniform.

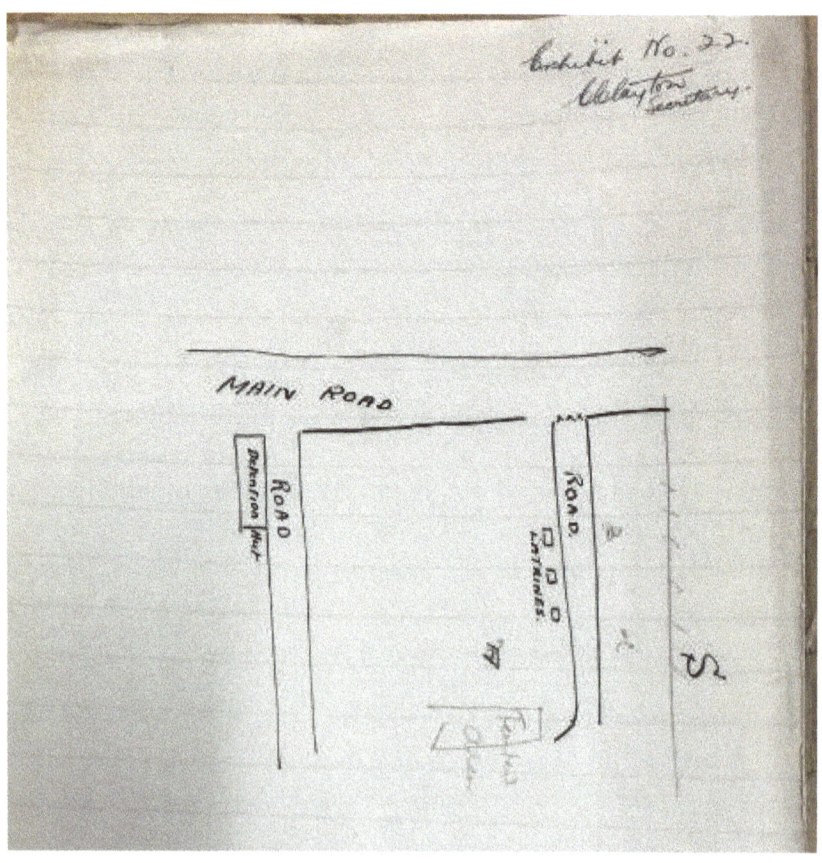

Exhibit 22. Sketch by Justice Simpson. POW Carmine Perugini (also known as Carmelo Perugini) marked A to show his position, B Bartoli and C Captain Waterston[18]

A Veritable Nero – Justice Simpson's Inquiry Commences

There are significant discrepancies in Waterston's evidence given relating to the shooting of Bartoli. The prisoners who went to Bartoli's aid and the medical staff who removed his clothing didn't find any bulky items or anything concealed on him. All of the prisoners and military personnel interviewed, except McDougall, contradict Waterston's evidence that a verbal warning was given and a warning shot was fired. Only one shot was heard. Waterston was unable to produce the spent cartridges from the shots fired from his .303 rifle and the homicide detectives were unable to find any bloodstains in the location near the fence where Waterston had said that Bartoli was shot. Bloodstains were only found in one location, the location where Bartoli was collected from by stretcher. The angle of the bullet wound entering on Bartoli's right-hand side was inconsistent with Waterston's position that he gave in evidence. Three prisoners saw Waterston approaching Bartoli after firing the shot from the south-west, not the south-east as Waterston had stated. A shot fired from the south-west would be consistent with Bartoli's wound.

Despite it being late in the day, the visibility was still good enough for prisoners to recognise both Bartoli and Waterston from their tents. The author visited the site of the shooting, which is still in a bushland setting, on the evening of 30 March 2018. The southern boundary road and the concrete foundation of the latrine featured in the photograph used as Exhibit 27 are still visible. The weather conditions were similar to the conditions on the day of the shooting. The light began to dim at around 6.30 pm (7.30 pm AEDT) but it was still possible to clearly recognise people and faces at a distance at that time. It wasn't until 6.45 pm (7.45pm AEDT) that the light began to dim, and visibility was reduced to a point where it would be difficult to identify a person.

Bartoli had been in the camp since December 1944. He worked in the quartermaster store alongside Australian military staff and was well known to Captain Waterston. It is hard to imagine that Waterston didn't recognise him that night.

In June 1946, Nora wrote to Rodolfo's parents in a letter that subsequently wasn't posted.

> My Dear Mr and Mrs Bartoli,
>
> Yesterday I received your kind letter and I feel how weak and fruitless must be any words of mine which should attempt to beguile you from your grief of a loss so overwhelming. But I cannot refrain from sending you our deepest sympathy for I know just what you are suffering.
>
> My father, mother, sisters and brothers loved him as a son and brother, and it was a severe blow when we learnt of his death.
>
> We are not satisfied with the supported cause of Rodolfo's death and my father and others are making exhaustive enquiries into it and have contacted Federal Parliament and the acting Prime Minister. The enquiry has begun with the general treatment of the POW. (At present cannot write too much in fear of this letter being intercepted.) My father wrote a full account to a POW who will see you personally when he goes back.
>
> I should like very much to write you a long epistle but my mind is very confused at present maybe in the future I shall be more able to express some of the beautiful memories, which I feel would give you a little comfort. Rodolfo always believed in God, therefore my dearest friends we must never forget this.
>
> Now I must close, so may God bless you all.
>
> Nora

CHAPTER 10

John Finn – Missing Iron Sheets and Stolen Goods

John (Jack) Finn's farm was located across the road from the camp. John ran a piggery and he and his wife Kitty had a small shop in a lean-to on the side of their house on Stud Road. When the Australian and American soldiers were in Rowville, they used to sell apples and lemonade to the soldiers.[1]

John Finn's name had come up several times during the inquiry. He appeared before Justice Simpson on 18 July 1946.

In the courtroom that morning was Mr Moloney, representing the Italian prisoners on behalf of the Swiss Consulate, Mr Sweeney, assisting Justice Simpson and Mr Minogue, representing Waterston.

Just prior to Finn being called to the witness box, Sweeney, Moloney and Justice Simpson discussed Finn's upcoming appearance. Sweeney alerted the commissioner that the topic of some missing iron sheeting from the camp would come up during Finn's evidence. Moloney explained, 'I am further informed by Mr Minogue – and I think it is common ground – that the tin of which Mr Finn and Detective McMennemin will speak, has no relation to the 110 sheets of tin from a demolished hut that were missing from the camp.'

Moloney told Justice Simpson that he would like to be excused from the courtroom during Finn's appearance. 'Before the witness goes into the box, I would like Your Honour to know that I propose to leave the court and not ask him any questions, for a reason which both Finn and I know in a professional capacity, and I would feel embarrassed by remaining. Something may arise which may embarrass both the witness and myself.'

Moloney's mysterious disappearance appears to be due to the fact that he had represented Finn at the Dandenong Magistrate's court two days earlier where Finn had been charged with, and was found guilty of, receiving stolen goods from the Rowville camp. Found in Finn's possession were sixteen tins of jam, fish and fruit. Finn was spared a custodial sentence due to his good reputation and was fined ten pounds. This information was not revealed during the inquiry.[2]

Once Finn appeared in court before Justice Simpson, he was asked about his arrangements with the camp. Finn explained that he had a contract to visit the camp two to three times a week to collect food scraps from the kitchen. He used the food scraps to feed his pigs. It was an arrangement set up with Captain Waterston's predecessor, Lieutenant Dunt, and had been in place for well over a year. When asked by Sweeney about iron sheeting from the camp that may have been relocated to his farm, he explained that he had eight sheets from the camp.

'Did you say anything to Captain Waterston about them?'
'No, I do not know that I did. I just asked him for them, if they were of any use.'

'Did you ask the captain if the sheets were of any use?'
'I probably did.'

'You had the advantage of being there. I am asking you to tell His Honour if you did ask the captain that?'
'I would say I did.'

'Did you, Mr Finn?'
'I think so.'

The commissioner then interrupted. 'Let us go back a bit. Did you take some sheets?'
'I took away those sheets that he gave me.'

'Did you take them away with somebody's permission?'
'I took them away with the captain's permission.'

'Before you took them and got his permission, did you speak to him about it?'
'Yes, I must have.'

'I think that follows, too, but what did you say?'
'I cannot recollect exactly what I said.'

'Not word for word, but tell us the effect of what you said.'
'I probably said, Are those of any use? or something like that.'

'Is that the best of your recollection?'
'Yes, something like that.'

'What did Captain Waterston say?'
'He said that they were not used, and that he would probably put them in the tip and I could have them.'

According to Finn, the eight iron sheets were used as part of the roofing on a piggery at his farm. The subject of missing iron sheets had been discussed in the inquiry a week earlier during Italian POW Enrico Quintavalle's interview, where he recounted that the day before the Coroner's Inquest in May, Waterston had assaulted him several times. Quintavalle had been working on Finn's farm and Waterston had heard that Quintavalle had been spreading rumours that Bartoli had been killed because he knew too much about the captain and the 110 missing corrugated iron sheets that had allegedly ended up on Finn's farm. Waterston forced Quintavalle to make a written statement stating that he had no knowledge of the reason for Bartoli's death. Quintavalle did, however, know of the missing sheets and had heard prisoners discussing them. A work party in the camp had been instructed to dismantle one of the camp huts and the iron sheets from the hut had gone missing. Quintavalle saw some iron sheets, about sixty or seventy, on Finn's farm when he started working there. Finn was building some huts for his pigs and Quintavalle was told there was about two more years' worth of construction work to do. He had only made a provisional building for small pigs.

Finn was then questioned by Mr Sweeney on how it came about that he was able to have three prisoners from the camp working on his farm. He was asked if he had approached Captain Waterston about having prisoners working on his farm.

'Yes, I asked him if I could get them or hire them – something to that effect.'

'What did the captain say when you asked him for the prisoners?'
'He got permission.'

'I'm not asking what he did, but what he said to you.'
'I do not know what he said.'

The commissioner asked Finn, 'Did he say you can have them or you will have to fill in a form or you will have to get permission?'
'He had to make some sort of arrangement or get some authority, I think he said.'

Sweeney continued, 'Did Captain Waterston tell you that it was in his power to grant your application?'
'No.'

'Are you confident about that?'
'Yes.'

John Finn – Missing Iron Sheets and Stolen Goods

'How long have you been confident of that?'
'He said he had to—'

Sweeney cut him off. 'My question is, how long have you been confident that the captain did not tell you it was in his power to grant your application?'
'I have always understood that he had to make further inquiries.'

'Did you not tell me this morning outside this courtroom that the captain told you that it was within his authority to grant your application?'
'No, I do not think so.'

'Do you think you might have?'
'I do not think I did, no.'

Finn maintained that he had difficulty remembering the details because he hadn't taken much notice and had been keen to get the prisoners working on the farm as his sows were coming into mating season.[3]

At a later session in the inquiry, Major Sandy, who was familiar with the correct procedures in allocating prisoners to farms as labourers, was asked what an officer should do if he was asked to provide prisoners for labour on his farm. 'The correct procedure would be to apply to his local National Service Officer, who would then forward the application of the farmer to the Deputy Director of Manpower, who would approve or deny the request. The request would then be forwarded to the army to check for any security concerns.'

Mr Sweeney asked, 'Was there authority for a prisoner of war commanding officer of a hostel to supply prisoners of war on request?'
'No.'

'May we take it, then, that if Captain Waterston supplied prisoners to Mr Finn without following the course you have said was the correct course, his action would be irregular?'

'Yes.'[4]

This was not the first time that prisoners had been working on local farms without going through the official channels. During Major Ruddock's February 1945 inspection of the camp, he followed up a complaint from a number of nearby farmers that one farmer had been using prisoners for picking tomatoes.[5]

Senior Detective William McMennemin visited Finn's farm on 5 April 1946 and was making inquiries about a large quantity of missing iron sheeting from the Rowville POW camp. Finn showed McMennemin the eight sheets of iron, which were full of holes and had been straightened, and told him that the captain had said that he could take them. McMennemin spoke to Waterston at the camp the following day. He said that he had had a long conversation with Waterston about the missing large quantity of iron sheeting (but there is no further information about this in the transcript). He also asked Waterston about the eight sheets that Finn had taken. Waterston told McMennemin that he had said that Finn had asked him about them, but Waterston had not told him that he could take them.

Senior Detective McMennemin gave evidence at the Dandenong Magistrate's court on 15 July 1946 where Finn was on trial for receiving stolen goods. The case had initially been heard on 6 May when two former Australian Army cooks from the POW camp were found to be in possession of stolen goods, eleven tins of jam and four tins of fish. One of the cooks was found guilty and fined six pounds, the second was found not guilty. The hearing was adjourned before Finn could finish giving his evidence because someone had approached the magistrate in the street outside the court during a break in proceedings. Finn's hearing continued in July. Finn told the court that he had been offered some tinned goods while at the camp but had refused the offer, but the cook placed the tins in his truck. He also said that, at Russell Street Police Station, a soldier and McMennemin had told him that he should say that he had paid for the items. Finn implied that he had been coerced into signing an untrue statement saying that he had paid a soldier for the tins. The magistrate said that it appeared improbable that a police officer would suggest that Finn say that he had paid for the goods. He was found guilty of receiving stolen goods belonging to the Commonwealth, knowing they had been stolen from the POW camp at Rowville, and received a fine. There was no further mention of the missing iron sheets.[6]

Later, at Captain Waterston's court-martial hearing, Quintavalle was questioned about the discussion with Mr Gearon prior to the Coroner's Inquest.

Quintavalle had been leaving work at Mr Finn's farm when Mr Gearon and two men approached him. Mr Gearon reassured him that he was a friend of Bartoli and wanted Quintavalle to tell him what had happened in the camp. Mr Gearon told him that the two men with him were policemen and that Quintavalle had nothing to be afraid of. Through an interpreter, Quintavalle went on to recount what he had told Mr Gearon.[7]

'I said about the shot that the camp was not in revolt; there was no revolution. He asked me if there was any mutiny in the camp. He asked me if one man had been shot. Gearon asked me whether Captain Waterston was hitting men in the camp. He asked me if I had seen some iron sheets. I said, "Yes, I saw some iron sheets." He said, "Do you think they are the iron sheets that disappeared from the camp a month ago?" And I answered, "I don't know. I saw some iron sheets but don't know whether they came from the camp."'

The defending officer asked Quintavalle, 'Did he also ask you if you thought that Captain Waterston had killed Bartoli, if he knew too many things about Captain Waterston?' Quintavalle replied, 'Yes.'

The defending officer put the question to Quintavalle, 'Did you think he killed Bartoli because he knew too much about him?'

Quintavalle replied, 'I don't know Captain Waterston killed Bartoli for that because Bartoli was not a particular friend of mine and I did not know what he knew about Captain Waterston.'

During Justice Simpson's inquiry, Waterston suggested that he thought that Mr Gearon was the source of the rumour about the missing iron sheets and alleged that Gearon had caused him problems within the hostel by welcoming prisoners to his farm. Ted Gearon had given evidence at the Coroner's Inquest and had spoken to the homicide detectives. Justice Simpson had considered calling Mr Gearon to give evidence but was of the opinion that Mr Gearon's evidence would be second-hand.

John Gearon had sent a written complaint to the authorities based on information that some of the prisoners in the camp had given him. Nora typed the letter for her father. He had been told that Captain Waterston was confiscating prisoners' possessions, including gifts and food given to them when they arrived at the camp or returned from working on farms. The prisoners had told him that Waterston was passing the confiscated items on to John Finn's shop across the road and he was then selling them at local markets and the Queen Victoria Market. The letter was sent just before Rodolfo's death. Nora had always wondered if the letter 'had some bearing on the matter'.[8]

CHAPTER 11

Justice Simpson – Captain Thomson and Major Ruddock

Captain Thomson was the Captain and Company Commander of the Prisoner of War Hostel Company and was based at the Murchison camp. Lieutenant Dunt had been initially placed in command at Rowville until Captain Thomson replaced him with Captain Waterston in February 1945. At this time, the number of prisoners had just increased from 100 to 150 and he had been concerned about some of the activities of the neighbouring civilians. Thomson felt that, with an increase in prisoner numbers and no increase in staff, an officer of higher rank was required to deal with the growing prisoner population and potential disciplinary issues.

Mr Sweeney asked Captain Thomson if he was familiar with the letter that formed part of the terms of reference for the inquiry. He responded that he was familiar with the statements in the letter. Mr Sweeney also asked if, during the course of his visits to Rowville, he had seen anything to support the allegations. He responded, 'Only in one case. In June last year (1945), we received a report that the prisoners had refused to go to work because a number of prisoners had been ill-treated by Captain Waterston. Major Sandy, second-in-command of the Murchison Prisoner of War Group, and I proceeded to Rowville, called all the prisoners on parade and asked why they had not gone to work.' Captain Thomson spoke to the prisoners through the camp interpreter,

Sergeant Heynemann. 'I told the prisoners that I would not consider anything till they went to work, and I ordered them into the trucks and called the camp leader with some three or four, who stepped out of the ranks, to remain behind. We went into the orderly room and, in company with Captain Waterston, Major Sandy conducted the inquiry.' Two of the prisoners who joined them in the orderly room had visible facial injuries, one with a cut lip and another with some sort of facial injury – Captain Thomson couldn't recall the specific details. The man with the cut lip had been found out of bounds by Captain Waterston and had refused to get onto a truck, so Waterston pushed him onto the truck, resulting in a cut lip. The second man had refused to go into his cell; Waterston pushed him into the cell, causing him to hit his face on the cell wall. 'The camp leader was informed that we did not, as a garrison unit, subscribe to rough handling of prisoners by officers and went away seemingly quite contented.'

According to Thomson, Major Sandy spoke to Captain Waterston afterwards and said, 'You are a big man and you may not know your own power. It is very ill-advised for you to lay your hand on a prisoner. You will find yourself in serious trouble if you do. If there is any laying of hands to be done on prisoners, let the camp leader do it.' Waterston assured Major Sandy that there would be no repetition of the incident.

The Rowville camp was an open camp; there were no gates or barbed wire fences. Captain Thomson explained that the prisoners were allowed on the main roads to the boundaries of the Rowville township. 'The prisoners were allowed to walk up and down the road and there was one entrance to the camp, the main entrance. The prisoners could move in the direction of Dandenong along the road to a bridge, and in the other direction north, they could move to another bridge. Westerly, they could move to another bridge; easterly, they were permitted to go quite a distance through the Lysterfield camp area.' Captain Thomson's records showed that in the previous nine months there had been thirty escapes. Twelve had been caught or handed themselves in and eighteen were still at large. On 18 February 1946, eight prisoners escaped from the camp and Captain Thomson went to Rowville to meet with Captain Waterston to try to address the issue of prisoners escaping, starting with the camp boundaries.

The commissioner responded to Captain Thomson's description of the eight prisoners escaping. 'Escaped is hardly the word – absconded, walked off.'

Captain Thomson continued, 'In company with the Company Adjutant, Lieutenant Purbrick, I went to Rowville and we conducted a search throughout the afternoon and the night in an endeavour to apprehend these prisoners, and we were unsuccessful. I then called a conference in Captain Waterston's office and I instructed Captain Waterston to alter the boundaries of the camp...I laid down a boundary which was well defined in the area.' The boundary was to be the internal road within the camp and inside the camp fence which loops around in a horseshoe shape. This boundary was to be in place at all times.

Captain Thomson was asked by Sweeney how the details of the new boundaries were communicated with the prisoners.

'Is there any standard method laid down by which orders should be promulgated to prisoners?'
'Yes, it is contained in the NSR (National Security Regulations) and the Geneva Convention, paragraph 20, I think.'

'That is a matter with which you are quite familiar as an expert?'
'Quite familiar.'

'Will you tell His Honour in substance how it should be promulgated?'
'The effect is that it must be transmitted to the prisoners in a language which they can understand.'

'In the work of prisoner of war groups, has anything in the way of standard practice grown up, oral or written or both?'
'Both, that is transmission of orders to prisoners.'

'Does that transmission consist of posting the notice in a language which the prisoners will understand?'
'Yes, but that has not proved very satisfactory.'

'Is the camp leader told to make an announcement in the language of the prisoners, conveying the sense of the order or regulation?'
'Yes, that is the more general practice.'

'Is it the practice to do both things?'
'Yes.'

The commissioner asked Thomson, 'You put a notice on the notice board outside the orderly room and the camp leader is told what the new order is, and told to tell his fellow prisoners?'
'That is the desirable way, but the reason the orders are transmitted verbally is that a number of Italian prisoners are illiterate in their own language and, when they are apprehended for breaking bounds or any other misdemeanour, they plead ignorance of the language and cannot read or write, so quite a habit has grown up to promulgate orders verbally, and with a good camp leader, all you have to do is tell him and he sees that his men know the orders.'

Thomson returned to the inquiry the following day and was asked some further questions from Mr Adami from the Swiss Consulate who appeared for the Protector of Italian Interests. He put some questions to Thomson about the communication to prisoners of the new camp boundaries.

'In regard to the order as to the camp boundaries, did you give any instruction as to how the prisoners were to be informed of that?'
'No. Captain Waterston was the Camp Commandant.'

Mr Adami pointed out to Captain Thomson that Captain Waterston had stated in evidence numerous times that after 6 pm the boundary was the road, yet Captain Thomson had stated that it was to be the boundary twenty-four hours a day. Adami continued, 'You realise that,

in reference to the shooting of the prisoner of war, the position of the boundary is very important?'
'I do, it is most important.'

Colonel Flannagan, representing the army, continued questioning Thomson on the camp boundaries.

'You said that you took down some orders in the camp and posted up the new ones?'
'Yes, on 7 April this year.'

'Were those orders fixing the new camp boundaries?'
'Yes. Captain Waterston went away on leave and I remained in charge of the hostel over the weekend. On the weekend, I determined that there would be no doubt about the boundaries in the future. I caused the camp leader – I do not know his name, but it was the present camp leader – to marshal every prisoner in the camp and have them marched round the area and shown their boundary.'

'Was this before or after the shooting?'
'After. I also drew up a certificate to the effect that all prisoners in the camp were conversant with the boundary and that all prisoners coming into the camp would be made familiar with the boundary by the camp leader. On that certificate, I drew a plan of the area and outlined in red the road and laid down the boundary.'

'Prior to the shooting, what orders were there which fixed the camp boundaries for the prisoners?'
'The order in the men's hut, drawn by Lieutenant Dunt, showed the area of the camp proper and the perambulating points beyond which the prisoners could not perambulate on the road. I took them down.'

Mr Sweeney interrupted, 'Did I understand you to say that the old notice which you took down in April of this year had been up before Captain Waterston's time?'
'Yes, since the inception of the hostel.'

'You destroyed it when you took it down?'
'No, I took it up to the office. I will make a search for it; it might be there.'

'Would it convey to a prisoner reading it alone, without the benefit of any other instructions, the belief that he was free to circulate within the points designed on that plan?'
'That would be the position.'

'And if a prisoner who had not heard any verbal promulgation were to have read that notice, it would have conveyed to him that he was free to move inside the perambulating points shown there?'
'Yes.'

Written Complaints

One of the criticisms of the camp administration had been that letters of complaint written to the Swiss Consul had not been passed on. Captain Thomson was asked by Mr Sweeney what the procedure was if a prisoner at Rowville wanted to write a letter of complaint to the Swiss Consul.

'The procedure adopted is that he goes to his camp leader and makes a request to write on his behalf to the Swiss Consul...there is nothing to stop a prisoner writing individually to the Swiss Consul, provided it is sent through the normal channels.'

'What would be the normal channels for such a complaint?'
'The normal channels are that the prisoner of war or camp leader writes a letter in Italian and hands it to the Prisoner of War Control Office who, in turn, sends it to Murchison to be recorded and forwarded to the Swiss Consul.'

The commissioner asked, 'It goes uncensored, I understand, and unopened?'

Thomson responded, 'It is sealed in a separate envelope and we keep copies. Translations are kept. The original letter in Italian goes in a separate envelope to the Swiss Consul.'

'It goes from the Prisoner of War Control Centre to Murchison so there may be a check and record?'
'Yes.'

'So, if a prisoner said he gave one to Captain Waterston and it did not go on, the record shows whether it did go on?'
'Yes, sir, at Murchison. We have recently innovated a very complete system of registration at the hostel.'

Mr Sweeney asked, 'When you say recently, how recently do you mean?'
'Within the last two months.'

This question was asked of Captain Thomson on 29 May 1946.

Conspiring

Captain Thomson had told the homicide detectives and stated during Justice Simpson's inquiry that a number of prisoners had conspired to give false evidence about the number of shots that had been fired when Bartoli was killed.

While exploring this subject, Mr Sweeney reminded Thomson of a letter of complaint that Scuma had written after the shooting of Bartoli, the letter that Thomson confronted Scuma about on the day of the Military Court of Inquiry. Mr Sweeney read out a passage from the translated letter.

> At 6.20 pm on 30 March 1946, the Prisoner of War Rodolfo Bartoli was quietly walking about within the camp area, which is marked by a common fence dividing the military area allocated to the prisoners of war and private property.

> At a distance of about twenty metres from the said fence, Bartoli was felled to the ground by a rifle shot in the abdomen.
>
> I was not far away and, after the explosion of the shot which I heard very distinctly, I saw Captain JW Waterston, Hostel Commandant, who, armed with a rifle, was walking towards his office. At the same time, I also saw Bartoli lying on the ground, and he was writhing and groaning in a pool of blood.[1]

Mr Sweeney asked Thomson, 'Scuma was removed from Rowville on the day following the shooting, was he not?'
'Yes, on the Sunday.'

'Scuma set out in the letter the version which you had said you came to believe the prisoners had agreed to concoct?'
'I do not follow you.'

'Would you agree that that sets out in substance the facts which you felt the prisoners had agreed among themselves to concoct and to swear falsely? He speaks of a shot and of a fence being the boundary. Do you agree with that?'
'Yes.'

'It strikes you now?'
'Yes.'

'Are you inclined to drop your concoction theory now?'
'No.'

'You would stick to it?'
'Yes.'

'You hold it as firmly as ever?'
'Just as firmly as ever.'

'Not more firmly?'
'Quite firmly.'

A discussion continued about whether Thomson had heard any of the news in the press or any of the evidence given at the inquiry by the Australian military personnel present on the night of the shooting who were also unclear on the camp boundaries, and who gave evidence that they only heard one shot that evening. The commissioner put the following question to him.

'Why did you not question the AMF personnel as to how many shots were fired and as to what orders they had received as regards to the boundary before the Thursday when you arrived at the conclusion that a conspiracy on the part of POWs was being concocted?'
'Because I cross-examined and questioned Sergeant Major McDougall, the only member of the AMF staff in that area. He assured me of the number of shots fired and the challenge. I accepted that as a fact.'

'If I tell you now that about twenty Italians have said they heard one shot that night and that some number, about half a dozen, AMF people have said they heard one shot, if I tell you that, and you accept it for the purpose of the question that evidence has been given on oath, do you still feel confident in your own mind that the story of one shot is a concocted piece of perjury? Do you still believe that?'
'Yes.'

Thomson was pressed on the origin of his suspicions. He had spoken to the new camp leader, Trucco, when they stopped briefly while he was driving him to Puckapunyal. Trucco had said that there were four prisoners who were conspiring to give false evidence about the number of shots fired but was unwilling to share their names.

Mr Sweeney continued questioning Thomson on the subject. 'But you were hot on the plot. You had something which confirmed your darkest suspicion. You were elated to know you were right.'
'I knew I was right.'

'You at least derived some satisfaction from knowing you were right; that was only human.'

'Yes.'

'And being human, you felt some satisfaction?'
'Yes, my suspicions were finally confirmed when he mentioned four.'

'Having got to that stage, the names of the conspirators were of keen interest to you, was it not?'
'Most interesting.'

'And you pressed Trucco for them, did you not?'
'No.'

'Why not?'
'Because I could not press him for them.'

'You could ask him earnestly, did you not do that?'
'I did not browbeat or threaten Trucco. I asked him if he could tell me who they were. But Trucco is an Italian prisoner of war. He is very fair and broad-minded, and probably truthful.'

'That is a tremendous character you give him.'
'Yes.'

'These conspirators were going to come along and perjure themselves?'
'Yes.'

'And you are a friend of Captain Waterston, are you not?'
'Yes.'

'Knowing that they were going to come along and perjure themselves, you believed they were going to do that to embarrass Captain Waterston, that was their object in your mind?'
'Yes.'

'Did it occur to you, that when they got into the witness box at the morgue, to say, "Is it not a fact that you conspired with other witnesses

to perjure yourself in regard to Captain Waterston?", that would have been a great help?'
'I put that in my statement to the police of the evidence I was to give at the morgue.'

The commissioner interrupted, 'That Trucco had informed you there were four?'
'That I had been informed there were four.'

Mr Sweeney continued, 'I am putting that you could not just ask prisoner of war A, "Is it not a fact that some prisoners have conspired to commit perjury against the captain?"'
'Yes.'

'But if you could say to an individual prisoner of war X, "Is it not a fact that you conspired with others to tell a perjured story?", that would have been very valuable to you?'
'I would have given anything to get those four names.'

'Did you not plead with Trucco to tell you?'
'Yes, I did.'

'Did you not tell him, "Look, Captain Waterston is being put into a position of jeopardy by these lies and I want you to assist the cause of justice", or something like that?'
'I certainly did not use those words.'

'Or something like it?'
'Yes, something along those lines. I tried to persuade Trucco to tell me the names of the four men.'

'And you tried again and again; it was most important?'
'Yes, most important.'

'And still you could not get anywhere with Trucco?'
'No.'

'He was prepared to tell you there was a conspiracy among the Italians?'
'In confidence.'

'He was prepared to do anything but not tell you their names?'
'I think Trucco is largely afraid of repercussions.'

'It was in your power to send Trucco practically anywhere, was it not?'
'Yes and no.'

'If you had gone to your seniors and said, "Trucco has been most helpful in exposing this conspiracy against Captain Waterston. I do not want him exposed to any consequences and I would like him sent to a place of complete safety", you could have arranged that?'
'No. I could have sent him to any one of twenty places at that time but each would be a prisoner of war camp.'

'There is an Italian officers' camp at Murchison?'
'They are still Italian prisoners of war.'

'Would not Trucco have been safe, and to enable you to clear up the conspiracy saga against your friend, Captain Waterston?'
'Even if we had moved Trucco to Myrtleford, we could not make Trucco divulge a thing. He is not a man you could coerce.'

'Knowing that, why did you try?'
'I treated Trucco very well and put the case to him in fairness that he might divulge the names to me, and I promised protection, but I still could not get the four names.'

The commissioner asked, 'Did he confirm your views that you must have formed by this time that the conspiracy was concocted in the early hours of Sunday morning?'
'I would take it so.'

'It must have been concocted, if it was concocted at all, must it not, in the darkness of Sunday morning?'

Justice Simpson – Captain Thomson and Major Ruddock

'Not necessarily.'

'You took Scuma away?'
'Scuma was not removed for that reason.'

'Scuma must have been a party, or have known about, or have been a clairvoyant, because he was telling the same story, and I understand from you he was at Murchison at lunchtime on Sunday.'
'He was at Rowville on Sunday.'

'He must have been either a party to it, or a clairvoyant, or telling the truth, because he was telling the same story as the conspirators.'
'Yes, I see your point.'
Mr Minogue added, 'Or telling a lie on his own account.'

The commissioner continued, 'A remarkable coincidence; he told the same two lies?'
'We had removed a number of prisoners to Puckapunyal.'

Mr Sweeney asked, 'You think that those prisoners who came from Rowville may have borne the tidings of this conspiracy to him at Puckapunyal?'
'It is possible.'

'And you think it is possible that Scuma adopted that and wrote a long letter of complaint about that?'
'That is a possibility.'

'Do you remember saying you told the police about this concoction?'
'In my statement to Detective Adam or Detective Petty, I told them.'

'You told them of this discovery you made?'
'Yes.'

'And you realised its importance when you told them?'
'Yes.'

'You made it just as clear to the detective as to His Honour today?'
'I just wrote my statement; it was not thrashed out at length as today.'

'No one cross-examined you?'
'No.'

'Fortunately, perhaps, but you did want to make your meaning clear to the detective?'
'I handed a copy to Captain Waterston's counsel.'

'You realised that this was the kingpin of Captain Waterston's case, apart from his own statement?'
'No.'

'That it was a very vital piece of information?'
'I thought it was important.'

'And you thought it was important to make it clear to the detective that these Italians had agreed among themselves to concoct a story which was false and to swear to it; that is what was important?'
'Yes.'

'And that is what you made clear to the detective?'
'I thought I did.'

'Let me read your statement on a material point. Will you agree that this is an accurate reading of your statement on this point: "I had contact with a PWI who kept me informed of the activities of the prisoners at Rowville after the night of 30 March 1946. This PWI informed me that a certain section of PWI were rehearsing a story to tell at the inquiry and had agreed to tell the same story. When Detective Adam asked any prisoner who had witnessed the shooting on the night of 30 March 1946 to step out of the parade, nine prisoners without hesitation stepped out. These prisoners were immediately removed from Rowville on my orders." Would you agree that this is a paragraph from your statement to the police?'

'No, that date – 30 March – is not correct. I did not move Trucco down until after that date.'

'You say, "I had contact with a PWI who kept me informed of the activities of the prisoners at Rowville after the night of 30 March 1946." Do you agree that that is a paragraph from your statement?'
'Yes.'

'And that is the language you chose to tell the detective, that these prisoners had concocted a false story and were going to perjure themselves in swearing to it?'
'Yes.'

'With a view to incriminating Captain Waterston?'
'Yes, that sounds very much like my statement.'

Captain Thomson was asked about his conduct during the Coroner's Inquest in May. Mr Moloney suggested to Thomson that he got 'a little bit excited' at the Coroner's Inquest. Moloney explained, 'Do you remember at the finish speaking to Mr Adami, and you threatened to punch Mr Adami's nose and you used the word "bloody" at that stage, did you not?'
Thomson replied, 'No.'

'You did not do that?'
'No.'

'Did you not say, "I have a good mind to do it now"?'
'No.'

'That is as true as the rest of your evidence, is it?'
'Yes.'[2]

Major Ruddock

Major Ruddock had served in both World War One and World War Two. He was the Inspector of POW Control Centres and Control Hostels and had visited the Rowville camp initially in February 1945, his last visit being on 17 January 1946. Major Ruddock's reports were presented as exhibits in the inquiry. The reports were in his handwriting and, at the end of each visit, would be handed to his superior officer, Colonel Peters, for processing. The reports were a form with defined fields to be filled in and room for general remarks.

Mr Sweeney asked Major Ruddock about the nature of his inspections.
'Generally, your duties were to carry out inspections of the administration of the camp?'
'Yes, a good general inspection of the camp, and take the report back to the AAQMG (Assistant Adjutant and Quarter Master General) for his information.'

Major Ruddock would arrive at the camp unannounced to make his inspections more effective. He would first check to see if the camp was clean and walk around the camp with Captain Waterston. He would check the office records, look through the quartermaster stores and the camp canteen, check the kitchens and speak to the camp leader.

'What would you say to the camp leader?'
'I would say, "How are things going, is everything all right?"'

'And what would the camp leader say? "Things are going well, everything is all right"?'
'That was the impression I got from him.'

'Did you inspect the detention barracks?'
'No, I did not go through detention.'

'You never went into the detention huts at all?'
'No.'

The commissioner asked, 'Did you know there was one?'
'I did not know there was one.'

Mr Moloney asked, 'That was not part of your duty?'
Ruddock responded, 'I was not asked that. Those were my instructions, given on the pro forma sheet.'

'And those questions were answered by you on return to Melbourne?'
'Yes, on some occasions I may have finished them earlier. I may have made them out at home before I went to the office the next day, so as to be able to hand the whole thing to my superior officer at once.'

Colonel Flannagan continued with further questions. 'On the visits you made to the camp at Rowville, were you ever told by the camp leader that prisoners were complaining of being slapped in the face and of ill-treatment by Captain Waterston?'
'No, not once.'

'You did not have any idea or any information to indicate to you as inspecting officer that prisoners were not being properly treated?'
'No, no indication whatsoever.'

'Did you hear anything to the effect that prisoners were sometimes locked up and given bread and water?'
'No, they never told me that at all.'

'Or that they were not getting proper meals?'
'No.'

'And you had no reason to suspect that if a prisoner was held for any reason, say, in arrest, he was not being treated in the way he should have been treated?'
'Quite right, nobody complained to me. As a matter of fact, I always saw the medical officer and had a long chat to him. On one occasion, I must have spent the best part of my lunch hour in his lunch hour having a yarn with him.'

'Do you remember his name?'
'There were two in my time: Galli and Musiari. I would have a long talk with the medical officer. I also went to the hospital to look at the patients and they never complained to me.'

The commissioner interrupted, 'When you come in the main gate of the Rowville camp, there is a hut on your right. Do you remember that?'
'Yes.'

'That is the detention barracks.'

After some further discussion about the major's inspections, Mr Minogue continued.
'Major, your inspection duty was purely of an administrative, routine nature?'
'My inspections were according to the pro forma I was given there on the general running of the camp.'

'You were not inspecting on behalf of the POWs?'
'No, I was inspecting on behalf of the AAQMG, Prisoner of War OC Area.'

The commissioner asked, 'Amongst the questions you were asked to report on, was there a copy of the Hague Convention there and a copy of the Adjutant-General's ruling made under National Security Prisoner of War Rules and a copy of the Prisoner of War rules themselves?'
'Yes.'

'And you bravely checked over that they were there?'
'Yes, made sure.'

'But did you make any attempt to see that they were being carried out?'
Major Ruddock did not answer the question.

'Did you not think, in addition to seeing that the documents were there, that you had an obligation to see that the contents of the documents were being obeyed?'
'I think I did. I saw everything.'

'Well, I hope you do not have to read some of the evidence here, it would hurt you to see how little you have done.'[3]

CHAPTER 12

Justice Simpson – Inquiry Finding

Justice Simpson's inquest ended on 16 August 1946 and his final report was completed on 27 August but it wasn't delivered to the Minister until October. The army expressed concern that, since censorship controls had now been removed on prisoner of war correspondence, that any prisoners 'obtaining knowledge of His Honour's criticisms would no doubt react unfavourably and would possibly cause disturbances or take action which may have unfortunate results.' Consequently, the report was marked as secret.[1]

In his report, Justice Simpson outlined the terms of reference of his inquiry based on the letter from Mrs Santospirito, gave details of the dates when the inquiry sat and those present in representing the various interests in the inquest. He provided some preliminary information about the history of the Rowville prisoner of war camp as well as the reporting structure for military personnel in the camp. The report then addressed each of the allegations in the terms of reference.[2]

Justice Simpson began by detailing the history of Captain Waterston's military service. He stated that he was satisfied that Captain Waterston was a very capable infantry officer 'who by sheer merit rose from a private soldier to a company commander.'

Did Captain Waterston assault prisoners of war or use physical force in relation to them?

Justice Simpson had 'no doubt that Captain Waterston not infrequently did assault prisoners of war by slapping them in the face with an open hand, on some occasions by punching them, and once or twice by kicking them.'

He went on: 'A very great volume of evidence was led from Italian prisoners of war that they had on occasions been slapped on the face by Captain Waterston. In the great majority of such witnesses I am satisfied that their evidence is true. In a few cases the evidence suggests that the slaps were really full punches, and on two occasions at least the prisoners bore evidence in the shape of bruises and a cut lip for some days after the assault…The Italian witnesses were corroborated by a number of Australian personnel.

'I regret to have to report that in my opinion these slaps and occasional punches were not given in just moments of irritation, but were part of Captain Waterston's methods of keeping discipline.'

Justice Simpson explains that evidence had been provided that Captain Waterston had been warned by Major Sandy from Murchison and by two of the Italian camp doctors that the way he physically treated prisoners was not appropriate or legal.

'Despite these complaints and more formal complaints, Captain Waterston continued to slap prisoners whenever he felt desirable up to the time when an announcement was published in the press that this present inquiry had been ordered.'

The transcript of evidence and Justice Simpson's report shows Captain Waterston openly admitted on a number of occasions to both slapping and punching prisoners.

On the question of Captain Waterston being under the influence of alcohol while on duty, Justice Simpson found no evidence that he was prepared to accept that Captain Waterston was ever intoxicated while on duty. He further clarified, 'By this I mean that on no occasion was Captain Waterston ever so affected by alcohol that he was not in full possession of all his faculties, but I am satisfied that very frequently he had indulged in alcohol to an extent that it became apparent to even casual observers that he had had drink. A large number of witnesses gave evidence as to their opinion of Captain Waterston's sobriety and their views differ all the way from "He was drunk" to "I thought I could smell liquor on him".'

Did Captain Waterston improperly take from any prisoner of war any articles of value belonging to the said prisoner of war?

A large number of prisoners gave evidence they had clothing and personal belongings taken from them. It did appear that Waterston had orders from his superiors to restrict the prisoners at Rowville to just the clothing they were issued. While at Murchison prisoners could purchase items from canteens and from time to time acquired clothing while employed on farms. Arriving at Rowville, these items would be confiscated. Any valuables found would be impounded and sent to Murchison headquarters where the item would be recorded, and a receipt sent to the prisoner. Unfortunately, this process was not clearly explained to the prisoners before they reached Rowville causing a great amount of ill feeling and the sense that Captain Waterston was stealing these items.

Justice Simpson criticised Captain Waterston in taking eleven shillings of token money from a prisoner, Marchiafava, and not recording that it had been taken. Also, Dutto had five bonds worth 500 lire taken from him. It was only after Justice Simpson's inquiry had commenced that three of the bonds were sent to Murchison to be securely stored, two of them had been lost. Justice Simpson believed that Waterston thought that the bonds were of little or no value and did not bother to send them to Murchison resulting in two of them being lost. 'I find Captain Waterston was grossly negligent in the manner in which he treated this man's property.'

Did Captain Waterston brandish or fire a revolver in or about the vicinity of the camp?

'Despite Captain Waterston's evidence to the contrary, I am satisfied that he did not infrequently brandish a revolver in and around the camp. I am also satisfied that on a number of occasions he fired a revolver in the air. These instances he does not deny.' Justice Simpson cited the following seven occasions where Captain Waterston had used his revolver.

Once when a convoy of prisoners had stopped at the Rowville camp to refuel, the captain asked the prisoners gathering around the truck to stand back and fired a shot into the ground when his order was not obeyed.

During an incident where some prisoners had refused to sign their pay sheets for their pay from the Italian Government, a physical altercation between one of the prisoners, Captain Waterston and one of the guards took place. They forced the prisoner outside and Captain Waterston fired a couple of shots into the ground.

While out on patrol, Captain Waterston found two prisoners on the main road outside the camp talking to some civilians in a car. He asked Sergeant Seymour to hold the civilians while he pursued the prisoners. Waterston fired two shots in the air.

In January 1946, a shot was fired in a detention cell. This may have been one occasion when the captain's actions were justified. The captain went to the cells to give the prisoners their blankets for the evening. In one cell the prisoners rushed the captain, he pulled out his pistol and fired a shot into the roof.

During a prisoner strike, possibly motivated by the way Captain Waterston had been treating them, the prisoners had congregated in the mess. The captain went in, ordered them to work and, when they refused, fired a shot into the mess roof.

One evening when the camp kitchens had closed, the captain found that a number of the prisoners had built small camp fires and were cooking coffee. The captain fired two shots.

The final occasion where shots were fired which Justice Simpson mentions was the night after the Military Court of Inquiry where Captain Thomson fired his pistol, breaking a light and putting a hole in the roof.

Was the food ample in quantity and of good quality?

Justice Simpson was satisfied that the food was ample and of excellent quality and, during the inquiry, he found that there were almost no complaints from the Italians about the food.

Was Captain Waterston's conduct connived at by his superiors or any of them?

Justice Simpson discussed Captain Waterston's failure to forward written complaints from a former camp leader. It was only after this prisoner had been relocated to Murchison and rewritten the complaint that it was recorded as being received at Murchison. Justice Simpson was confident that the letter 'must have come to the eyes of some official at Murchison.' Justice Simpson said, 'This letter was in such terms that it should have caused an investigation.' Justice Simpson was also satisfied that Captain Thomson knew of certain irregularities that were going on in the manner in which prisoners were given short sentences of detention at Rowville and connived at such conduct.

On the circumstances resulting in the death of Rodolfo Bartoli Justice Simpson wrote:

Bartoli was shot by Waterston at around 6.30 pm on the 30th of March.

Waterston gave two accounts to the Victorian police. During the inquiry, he claimed privilege to refuse to answer any questions in relation to the shooting on the grounds that such questions may incriminate him.

Justice Simpson found:

> I have to report that Bartoli was killed by a bullet from a .303 military rifle fired by Captain Waterston at somewhere towards 6.30 in the evening of March 30. The bullet entered Bartoli's body slightly to the right of the centre line of the right groin and left the body through the left buttock, the points of entrance and exit being approximately level one with the other. The spot where Bartoli fell was about 75 feet from the centre of the southern road within the camp and about 396 feet from the fence forming the perimeter of the camp. The area where Bartoli was shot consists of a semi-cleared area in which there are a number of tall trees interspersed with some saplings and undergrowth but in the main well cleared. At the time of the shooting the light was rapidly fading but it was not yet dark.
>
> At the time of the shooting Bartoli was dressed in the ordinary outer burgundy-coloured garments of a prisoner of war and apart from the reference in Captain Waterston's statement to a bulky object I have been unable to find any evidence to suggest that he was carrying or had anything either in his hands or under his tunic. A large volume of evidence was called as to the number of shots fired and I have arrived at the conclusion that only one shot was fired by Captain Waterston. There was a considerable controversy before me as to whether the area where Bartoli was shot was or was not out of bounds to the prisoners after 6 pm. I have no hesitation in reporting that so far as the prisoners had been informed it was not out of bounds and that the prisoners had been instructed that the boundary of the camp was the fence around the perimeter.

Justice Simpson – Inquiry Finding

> Following on Bartoli's death his personal effects were parcelled up. It was found then that in his suitcase which at the time of the shooting was still in the hut where he resided was two pounds Australian money and a number of private souvenirs and papers together with all his clothing.
>
> One other fact of importance. Bartoli had made the acquaintance of an Australian girl whom he hoped someday to marry and was in the habit apparently of visiting her without authority as he had obtained possession of a bike which he hid in the scrub outside the fence but not in the direction in which he was walking at the time he was shot.
>
> I am not satisfied that Bartoli intended to leave the camp that night either temporarily or in an attempt to escape.

Justice Simpson found the administration of the Rowville camp to be extremely unsatisfactory. He placed the blame for this on Captain Waterston, Captain Thomson and Major Ruddock and criticised two main areas of the administration, the methods of inflicting punishments awarded to prisoners of war and the method by which just complaints of prisoners of war, and in particular the camp leader, were neither forwarded nor redressed.

In the matters of discipline and punishment, Justice Simpson reported:

> I have to report that Captain Waterston in breach of his duty on a large but unascertainable number of occasions held POW in the detention cells without any form of trial and without recording the fact that these prisoners had been either convicted or punished and that he illegally caused a large number of prisoners of war who had been convicted and sentenced to varying terms of detention to be placed on a diet of bread and water for the greatest part of their sentences.

There are regulations for what and how long a prisoner can be detained, how detention is recorded and their food requirements. The maximum period of detention that a commanding officer can give to a prisoner is twenty-eight days. If a disciplinary issue occurs while the prisoner is in detention, the commanding officer can inflict a punishment of a No. 1 scale diet for a period not exceeding three days. This diet consists of one pound of bread and water. Justice Simpson found that Captain Waterston, in the majority of cases, ordered or permitted the men to be kept on a No. 1 diet for considerable periods of time and this was not for offences committed in detention but as part of punishment for the original offence.

Corporal McCarthy, whose duty it was to attend to the prisoners in detention, told the court that he was instructed by Captain Waterston to give the prisoners bread and water for three days and a full meal on the fourth day, then to return to the menu of bread and water for the following three days.

In the manner of dealing with official complaints of prisoners of war, Justice Simpson wrote:

> I have to report that Captain Waterston systematically attempted to prevent any prisoner of war from making a formal complaint in such a manner that it would reach Captain Waterston's superiors.

The Geneva Convention, to which both Italy and Australia are signatories, states that prisoners of war have the right to notify military authorities of any complaints they have. They also have the right to contact the protecting power to address their complaints. Any petitions or complaints must be transmitted immediately.

In his report, Justice Simpson gave three examples of letters of complaint not being dealt with appropriately. One letter of complaint was from Sergeant Parisi, the former camp leader, which was written in June 1945 and should have been referred to the Swiss Consul, the Red Cross Delegate and the Apostolic Delegate. He outlined in the letter which prisoners were assaulted by Captain Waterston and the Sergeant Major.

'The letter was handed to the captain in the morning. The captain had translations prepared of it and called me in the afternoon. He asked me whether I was refusing to carry on as camp leader because in the letter I pointed out that I could not carry on the camp leadership. I said I was not refusing but was relinquishing my position of camp leader. He said that I would have to go to prison because I was refusing to carry on as camp leader. Then they put me into prison.'

A record book of all letters is kept at Murchison containing columns showing how the letter is dealt with. The book showed that Parisi's letter was received but there is no indication of any further action. Justice Simpson was 'satisfied that some person in Murchison camp deliberately refrained from making the proper entries in relation to this letter and I can only conclude that it was ultimately destroyed. It certainly never reached the Swiss Consul.'

Justice Simpson continues, 'No words are too strong with which to criticise this action. I am quite satisfied that Parisi was sent to detention simply as a method of preventing the petition being forwarded…I am satisfied that the attempts to prevent Parisi's letter reaching higher authorities was not a solitary instance.'

Justice Simpson quotes a sergeant interpreter from the camp who gave evidence: 'In substance, they were complaints about alleged ill treatment…Captain Waterston persuaded the prisoners to withdraw their letters, not to send them on. They all agreed to withdraw their letters with the exception of one man…he said he would not withdraw it and insisted that he would not withdraw it, and finally he was dismissed from the office. I was sent after him a moment later to take him back to the office where he was told that he was under arrest for insolence…The captain said, as I remember it…"Don't forget that if this letter goes on you will still be here and I will still be here." The prisoner replied, "I am a soldier"…Later [the captain] told me a deputation had come and had told him that they had persuaded this man to withdraw the letter. I do not know whether he was released that night or the next morning.'

Justice Simpson was clear in his report that both Major Ruddock and Captain Thomson were responsible for Captain Waterston's conduct. Major Ruddock was employed to inspect the prisoner of war camps. His inspections of the Rowville camp were infrequent and at irregular intervals. Justice Simpson went on to say, 'If this officer had been at all competent in performing his duties he must, I think, have discovered many of the irregularities that have been brought out by this inquiry. He would, for instance, have discovered that there were very few records of punishment in the diary which Captain Waterston was required to maintain. If he ever visited the detention barracks and asked for complaints from the prisoners kept in detention, I am satisfied he would have been put on notice that something was wrong. In point of fact, he said in evidence that he did not know that there was a detention cell at Rowville. Through this officer's inefficiency, it appears to me that Captain Waterston was able to continue in his irregular management of this camp over a long period.'

Justice Simpson then addresses the issue of Captain Thomson. Captain Thomson was the officer directly in charge of Captain Waterston. 'This officer gave a very considerable body of evidence and I have no hesitation in stating that he was a witness who had no regard for the truth.' Waterston had said during the inquiry that he had told Thomson about the short detention arrangements. Thomson either knew about it, or should have known about it, through his own inspections and inquiries. Justice Simpson was satisfied that Captain Thomson and Lieutenant Purbrick had taken Scuma, the former camp leader, around the camp on the day of the Military Court of Inquiry 'and attempted to induce Scuma to say that the camp boundaries were the roads within the camp.' Justice Simpson didn't accept Thomson's evidence that he had arranged for the Italian prisoner, Lieutenant Trucco, to spy on the Rowville prisoners and uncover a plot to give false information at the inquiry.

Justice Simpson – Inquiry Finding

Justice Simpson concluded: 'I have to report that, in my opinion, the maladministration of Rowville camp was caused in part by Captain Waterston having been called upon to do more work than one officer could possibly do, and I am of the opinion that it is most desirable that, if the camp is to continue with its present establishment of prisoners of war, there should be at least two commissioned officers put on staff. I am of the opinion that Major Ruddock, Captain Thomson and Captain Waterston should be relieved of their appointments immediately.'

Addressing the issues arising from Justice Simpson's inquiry, the Coroner's Inquest and the Military Court of Inquiry, the Army Director of Legal Services recommended the following actions on 10 October 1946.

In view of the two findings, an open finding at the Coroner's Inquest and that the Military Court of Inquiry was of the opinion that Captain Waterston, in firing on the said PWI, acted properly in the execution of his duty, no further action was warranted on this issue.

The Army Directory of Legal Services recommended that the following nine charges be laid against Captain Waterston and a court-martial hearing was scheduled for 16 December 1946.

> Committing a civil offence – On 30 March 1946 assaulted Silvano Viviani by slapping him on the face and kicking him in the buttocks.

> Committing a civil offence – On 14 May 1946 assaulted Enrico Quintavalle by slapping him in the face.

> Neglect to the prejudice of good order and military discipline in that he at Rowville on 21 July 1945 when as Control Officer at Rowville Prisoner of War Control Hostel having taken from one Giovanni Dutto, an Italian prisoner of war, five interest bearing Italian bonds, each of 500 lira face value, neglected to take proper care of the said bonds so that two of the said bonds were lost.

Conduct to the prejudice of good order and military discipline at Rowville in April 1945 [when] he improperly discharged a firearm in the prisoners of war mess hut at the Rowville Prisoner of War Hostel.

Conduct to the prejudice of good order and military discipline at Rowville on 18 December 1946 [when he] improperly discharged a firearm in a detention cell at Rowville Prisoner of War Control Hostel.

Conduct to the prejudice of good order and military discipline at Rowville on a date unknown in December 1945 [when he] improperly discharged a firearm outside the orderly room of the Rowville Prisoner of War Hostel.

Conduct to the prejudice of good order and military discipline at Rowville on date unknown in December 1945 when [as] Control Officer in charge of Rowville Prisoner of War Control Hostel [he] placed Amedeo Cacciagrano an Italian prisoner of war under his control in detention without trial.

Conduct to the prejudice of good order and military discipline at Rowville on 30 March 1946 when [as] Control officer in charge of the Rowville Prisoner of War Control Hostel [he] placed Silvano Viviani an Italian prisoner under his control in detention without trial.

Conduct to the prejudice of good order and military discipline at Rowville 12 June 1945 when as Control Officer in charge of the Rowville Prisoner of War Control Hostel he received a written complaint from Giuseppe Parisi an Italian prisoner of war under his control then acting as Camp leader addressed to the Consulate of Switzerland, Melbourne failed to forward the said complaint to the Consulate of Switzerland Melbourne or to take any other proper action in respect thereof.

It was pointed out that when considering these charges, it should be considered that Captain Waterston was grossly overworked, he had a previous good work history but a lack of experience in work of this nature and, in some instances, had the tacit concurrence in general of his actions by his superiors.

The following two charges were laid against Captain Thomson with a court-martial hearing scheduled for 23 December 1946.

> Conduct to the prejudice of good order and military discipline in that at Murchison on or about March 1945 when Company Commander of the Prisoner of War Control Hostel Company concurred in the practice of Captain JW Waterston Control Officer in charge of the Rowville Prisoner of War Control Hostel, a part of the said Company placing prisoners of war under his control in detention without charging the said prisoners of war.

> Conduct to the prejudice of good order and military discipline at Rowville on 5 April 1946 improperly discharged a firearm in the officers' mess at Rowville Prisoner of War Hostel.

The memo is rather lenient on Major Ruddock and notes that he had already been relieved of his appointment. It noted that although his investigations at the camp were apparently incomplete due to him not knowing of the existence of the detention cells, he was meticulous at completing the pro forma paperwork and possibly not suited to the job of inspecting prisoner of war camps. The memo recommended that no further action be taken.

CHAPTER 13

Courts Martial and Major Ruddock

CAPTAIN WATERSTON FACED NINE CHARGES AT THE HEARING. Two related to assaults on prisoners, one related to neglecting to take care of a prisoner's money, three related to the discharge of firearms, two related to detaining prisoners without trial and one for failing to pass on a complaint to officials. His trial took place at Flemington on 16, 18, 20 and 21 December 1946. He pleaded not guilty to all nine charges. Sixteen witnesses, including Captain Waterston, were called to give evidence.[1]

The Herald, Monday 16 December 1946

None of the charges were related to the shooting of Rodolfo Bartoli and, at the beginning of the hearing, the defence raised the issue that a number of articles had been published in *The Age* and *The Argus* about the upcoming court martial and that it was as a result of the inquiry into the shooting of an Italian POW. The defence pointed out that the charges did not relate to the shooting at all and that the person quoted in the paper would be at risk of contempt of court but was confident the court and the outcome of the hearing would not be affected by this story.

The Argus, Wednesday 18 December 1946

> **Two Captains to be Tried**
> In *The Argus* of December 13 we published a telegram from Canberra under the above heading, reporting that two Australian Army captains would be court-martialled as a result of a report of Mr Justice Simpson on the alleged shooting of an Italian prisoner of war at Rowville internment camp, Victoria. One of the officers, Captain JW Waterston, has taken exception to the paragraph, and wishes it to be made clear that the charges against him in connection with the Rowville internment camp, with which the court-martial is dealing, are not related in any way to the shooting of the prisoner of war referred to.

Witnesses involved in the incidents relating to each of the nine charges were called and interviewed.

When it came to the incident involving the assault of Quintavalle, Captain Waterston said, 'I did not at any time strike him. I think it was impossible to strike him while sitting in a truck. I was standing on the ground by the truck. I went past and spoke to him. He did not hear me and I touched him over the shoulder. It was all I could do over the tailboard of the vehicle. I drew his attention and told him I wanted him in the office. He came in with me.' In the office, Waterston and Quintavalle discussed the rumour being spread about Bartoli and the missing iron sheets. Waterston said that Quintavalle refused to comment. 'I told him I would get it out of him one way or another. I did slap him once and I shook him. He subsequently did make a statement and all that talk died down immediately afterwards.'

The defence put it to Waterston that Sergeant Holtham, who was present in the room at the time, said in evidence that Captain Waterston struck Quintavalle multiple times.

'On the night that you saw Quintavalle before the inquest on the following day, you say you slapped him only once?'
'I do.'

'Would you deny it if somebody else said that you did it more than once?'
'I would.'

'You would say that Sergeant Holtham was completely inaccurate on the matter?'
'Definitely.'

'Now you realise that Quintavalle was saying something which, if true, would not have reflected very well on yourself?'
'I did not take that angle at all.'

'On your own evidence, was not Quintavalle saying this: Captain Waterston killed Bartoli because Bartoli knew too much about those sheets that were going from the camp?'
'That is what he said, yes.'

'And he was saying that on the night before the inquest?'
'Not that I know of.'

'And you don't realise now that, by slapping him on that night, you were doing a very foolish thing?'
'Nothing of the sort.'

'The reason you slapped him was to get the truth from him?'
'Exactly.'

'Doesn't it strike you that when you are slapping a person to get him to say something that you want him to say, it is just the way not to get the truth?'
'No, in this case it was not.'

'From your knowledge of military law and your experience of sitting on courts-martial you must have known that a statement to be of any value must be free and voluntary?'
'Yes, that is correct.'

'And you know that also from your experience, that British law takes a very poor view of statements that are not free and voluntary?'
'I know that.'

'And yet on that night before the inquest, you slapped Quintavalle in order to get a statement from him?'
'I did.'

'And that statement that he was making would have supplied a motive to put a very serious implication on Bartoli's killing as far as you were concerned?'
'Yes, I suppose it would have.'

'Do you still say that it was not a foolish thing to do?'
'Certainly, I don't think it was.'

'Even supposing that Quintavalle was telling a pack of lies do you think it was wise for you as commandant to maul him on the night before the inquest?'
'He was not mauled.'

'Well, you slapped him.'
'I don't think I did any damage.'

The Judge Advocate inquired, 'What was the statement?'
'The statement was to the effect that I had shot Bartoli.'

'I realise that. What was the statement that you were getting from Quintavalle?'

'That statement I intended to use because I fully believed that the people around there who started that story intended to use it against me and I wanted the evidence in a statement.'

'You wanted to use that for your own defence?'
'Exactly.'

Captain Thomson was later called as a witness and was caught out several times contradicting previous evidence that he had given. One of the charges which he gave evidence for was the occasion when Captain Waterston fired his pistol into the roof of the mess hall where striking prisoners had gathered in June 1945. Prisoners had been complaining about Captain Waterston mistreating them. They had refused to go to work and they had demanded to speak to a senior officer. Captain Thomson and Major Sandy from Murchison came to Rowville to help resolve the situation. They both gave prisoners the order to return to work and told the camp leader that Major Sandy would conduct a thorough investigation and ordered a truck for the men to go to work.

'I understand you and Major Sandy put them into the trucks at pistol point?'
'I do not think that would be correct. We were both armed, certainly.'

'Did you have a pistol out when you were putting the prisoners of war into the truck?'
'I did have occasion to draw a pistol but I did not remember drawing it on that occasion. I do not know whether I drew it or not.'

'What about Major Sandy?'
'I could not say.'

'Did you see him draw a pistol?'
'I cannot remember.'

'Was it a fact that, when you explained everything to the prisoners of war, they seemed happy?'
'I explained nothing.'

'But you explained to them through the camp leader that their complaints would be investigated?'
'That is correct.'

'That seemed to put them in a fairly happy frame of mind?'
'I don't know. The camp leader ordered them into the trucks.'

'And they obeyed his orders?'
'Yes.'

'At that time Major Sandy went down, is it a fact that he told Captain Waterston to be very careful about laying his hands on prisoners himself?'
'That is true.'

'He told Captain Waterston that he was a very big man and probably did not know his own power?'
'Major Sandy stated that in the inquiry. I cannot recall the words or conversation but I can recall him saying that at the inquiry.'

The Judge Advocate inquired, 'You only gave evidence of what you heard him say. You did not give any evidence about it yourself at the Rowville inquiry?'
'I don't think I was asked.'

The prosecuting officer continued. 'Do you remember saying this to Mr Sweeney at the inquiry? The camp leader was informed that we did not, as a garrison unit, subscribe to the rough handling of prisoners by officers and he went away seemingly quite contented. After that, Major Sandy spoke to Captain Waterston and said, "You are a big man and may not know your own power. It is very ill-advised to lay your hands on a prisoner. You will find yourself in serious trouble if you do. If there is any laying of hands to be done on prisoners, let the camp leader do it."'

The Judge Advocate asked again, 'Did you say that at the inquiry? Did you give that evidence?'
'Those are my principles.'

'Did you give that evidence?'
'Yes, I did.'

The prosecuting officer interjected, 'That statement is true, is it?'
'The statement is true.'

'How was it that you had forgotten about it a moment ago?'
'I had not forgotten about it.'

'I asked you whether you had given any evidence about what Major Sandy said and you said all that you knew about it was Major Sandy said it at the inquiry.'
'I said I could not recollect the words used at the time. That is what I meant.'

'You did recollect him saying something like that?'
'Yes.'

'Was it a fact that after that time you gave some sort of instructions that a patrol vehicle was not to go out with one officer and a driver in it?'
'That is correct.'

Captain Waterston pleaded not guilty to all charges and was found not guilty of all but the second charge, a civil offence: common assault by slapping Enrico Quintavalle in the face. He was sentenced with a reprimand for the charge of common assault.

Captain Thomson's Court-Martial Hearing

Captain Thomson's court-martial hearing was held at Flemington on 23 and 24 December 1946. Four witnesses appeared at the hearing. Captain Thomson wasn't questioned at all during the hearing. He faced two charges: one for concurring in the practice of detaining prisoners without charge and one for improperly discharging a firearm in the officer's mess on the night of the Military Court of Inquiry.[2]

Captain Waterston was the main witness interviewed for most of the two days of Thomson's court martial. The court found that Thomson had no case to answer on the first charge, which stated that at Murchison on or about March 1945 he had concurred with Captain Waterston in the practice of placing prisoners of war in detention without charging them. The court found that with the date of the charge being so vague, it was not possible to identify a single, relevant example where there was evidence of a discussion taking place and prisoners being kept in detention without charge. There was difficulty with the vague date since Captain Thomson was not company commander until May 1945 and that this incident may have occurred during that period when Thomson wasn't company commander; therefore, he could not have been responsible even if the discussion had taken place. Thomson was found not guilty of this charge.

The court moved on to the incident of the firing of pistols in the mess hall on the evening of 5 April 1946.

The prosecution began by interviewing Captain Waterston.

'Captain Waterston, do you remember attending a dinner in the mess at Rowville with Captain Thomson and Major Archer?'
'Yes.'

'Do you know what date that would have been?'
'Possibly a week following the shooting of Bartoli.'

'And that occurred on?'
'30 March.'

The Judge Advocate asked, 'What year?'
'"46."

The Prosecution continued, 'Who was present in the mess that evening?'
'Major Archer, Captain Thomson, myself and a lady.'

'About what time of evening did you have dinner?'
'I don't know what time it was. It was dark but I don't know what time we had dinner.'

'Were any firearms discharged in the mess that evening?'
'I heard a shot fired in the mess that evening.'

'How many shots?'
'One.'

'Did you fire that shot yourself?'
'No.'

'Who fired the shot?'
'I don't know. I thought Captain Thomson did, but I don't know that he did fire it.'

'Why did you think Captain Thomson fired it?'
'When I turned round, Captain Thomson was standing at the table and the pistol was on the table. I thought he had fired it, but I don't think he did now.'

'What has caused you to change your opinion?'
'I think I changed my opinion shortly afterwards. I think the shot was fired from a heavier pistol than he had.'

'Did the lady fire the shot?'

'She did not.'

'Did you see Major Archer fire the shot?'
'No.'

'What first drew your attention to the shot?'
'The sound of it.'

'In what direction did the shot go?'
'I don't know. I presume it would be the roof, but I don't know.'

'Where were Captain Thomson and Major Archer respectively standing when the shot was fired in relation to you?'
'They were not, actually. Major Archer was sitting at a table and Captain Thomson was half-standing and half-sitting. I was standing at the door of the mess with my back to him.'

'You are not sure that there was only one shot fired?'
'Only one that I remember. I left the mess immediately. I don't know what happened.'

'Do you know how many firearms there were in the mess that evening?'
'I think three, but I would not be sure of that. I gave my pistol to Captain Thomson to lock up for me.'

'For how long after the incident did you think Captain Thomson fired the shot?'
'I don't know.'

'Have you had any conversation with Captain Thomson about the incident?'
'Quite a lot.'

'What was the substance of the conversation that you had with him?'
'Concerning the firing of the shot. I don't know what it was. I stated that I thought Captain Thomson fired the shot and he objected and said he did not.'

'At the time of the inquiry to which the learned Judge Advocate has referred, who did you think had fired the shot at that time?'
'I believed at that time that Major Archer fired the shot.'

'And since the date of the inquiry until today, have you always held that belief?'
'I have never thought anything more about it. I have always thought that since then.'

'Have you thought that Major Archer fired the shot during the last week or so?'
'I have not had occasion to think about it until this case came up.'

'What time was that. What time do you mean by that?'
'Possibly about three weeks ago.'

'Three weeks ago, what was your opinion as to which officer fired the shot?'
'Same as it is now. I believed that Major Archer fired the shot.'

Waterston was then cross-examined by the defending officer. 'This dinner at the mess at Rowville, was it an ordinary meal?'
'Yes, an ordinary meal.'

'Two officers, Captain Thomson and Major Archer?'
'That is correct.'

'The Major, of course, he was an officer sent down from LHQ [Land Headquarters] to make an inquiry into these very matters which have been before the court?'
'That is correct.'

'He did in fact make a report on these matters?'
'He was living there for a week and made a report.'

'He exonerated you all?'
'He did.'

'He fancied himself as a pistol shot?'
'I do not know.'

'Was there any discussion about his prowess as a pistol shot?'
'I think the discussion was about the relative merits of British and Yankee equipment.'

'You had a pistol, all three of you were armed?'
'That is correct.'

'And I suppose, having dinner, you had taken the pistols to the mess with you?'
'We had to carry them; that was all.'

'Did you put them on the table or in your holster?'
'There was one on the table and one hanging over a chair.'

'I suppose dinner lasted for a fair while? You were talking and discussing things for a fair while?'
'It may have lasted a while. I doubt it.'

'You are quite sure there was not discussion about your prowess as a pistol shot?'
'There may have been. I do not remember it.'

'You are a very good pistol shot yourself?'
'I would not say that.'

Captain Waterston was then asked a number of questions by the Judge Advocate. He explained that he was standing at the mess door helping the lady on with her coat and he turned around when the shot was fired.

'When you turned around, you have told us Captain Thomson was part-sitting and part-standing near a table with a pistol in his hand, is that right?'
'Yes.'

'Where was Major Archer?'
'Sitting beside Thomson.'

'Which way was the pistol facing?'
'It was on the table. I cannot remember where it was facing. The butt was towards Thomson; I think; on a separate table with the butt towards Thomson.'

'What led you to believe that Captain Thomson fired the shot?'
'The fact that it was not a .38. It was a .45. I thought at the time Major Archer was in possession of the .45.'

'You turned around immediately you heard the shots?'
'No, not immediately. In about a second, I suppose.'

'When you last saw Major Archer, what was he doing?'
'Standing at a table.'

'Did he have a pistol in his hand?'
'I do not know.'

'Did you see him with a pistol in his hand?'
'I did not see him with a pistol in his hand.'

'Did you see Captain Thomson with a pistol in his hand that night?'
'Previously I did.'

'When you last saw him before the shot was fired, did he have a pistol in his hand?'
'No, sir.'

'Up to the time you got up to leave the mess, you were discussing the question of firearms?'
'Yes.'

'Where did you next see Captain Thomson after that night? First of all, did you see him again later that night after you escorted the lady from the mess?'
'I might clear up the position. I was on leave, Major Archer was having an investigation. I left the camp and Major Archer said, "I want you for about half an hour." I was in Melbourne. I took the lady to dinner with me and had dinner, cleared up a few details, had dinner and I left straight away and didn't return until Monday.'

The prosecuting officer then said, 'I propose to lead other evidence to the effect that Captain Waterston has given evidence differing from this at a very recent occasion and after the court having heard that, I propose to put it to the court as a basis for asking the court to deem Captain Waterston as a hostile witness in this case and permit me to cross-examine him on the new evidence that has been led.'

The Judge Advocate addressed Captain Waterston, 'You appreciate Captain Waterston, don't you, that if you give different evidence on previous occasions, you may find yourself in difficulties?'
Waterston answered, 'I appreciate that, sir.'

'Have you given evidence regarding this matter on oath on a previous occasion?'
'I have, sir.'

'When?'
'I believe at the inquiry.'

'Is it your belief that the evidence today corresponds with the evidence on that occasion?'
'To best I can remember it, yes.'

The prosecutor said at this point, 'My actual reference is to the evidence Captain Waterston gave at his own trial last week on this point.'

Captain Waterston's testimony from his court-martial case, which was held during the previous week, was then read from the transcript.

> 'At the dinner party, Captain Thomson and a major present indulged in some shooting in the mess?'
> 'I don't know about the major.'
> 'What about Captain Thomson?'
> 'I saw him fire a shot.'

Waterston was then asked, 'Were you asked who fired the shot?'
'Yes, sir.'

'And you said Captain Thomson?'
'Yes, sir.'

'Was that your belief at the time?'
'No, sir.'

'I want you, perhaps before answering that question, to remember giving false evidence on oath is a very serious offence.'
'I made a mistake, sir. I was asked suddenly that question by the prosecutor.'

'You have not believed it ever since?'
'No, I have not believed it. There may have always been a certain amount of doubt in my mind.'

The Judge Advocate said, 'In fairness to you, I think I should say that you have not only a duty but you have sworn to give evidence and to tell the truth and the whole truth. I said to you this morning that one can understand the embarrassing circumstances in which you are placed, but that doesn't relieve you from your duty or from the possible consequences of you committing perjury. You have heard the evidence which you have given on the last occasion and you remember the evidence that you have given today. Do you remember saying that on Friday you saw Captain Thomson fire the shot?'

'I don't remember saying that, but quite probably did say that.'

'Was that true?'
'No, sir.'

'Do you remember, when you gave your evidence on Friday, you did not know whether Major Archer fired the shot?'
'Candidly, sir, I did not know about either of them, who fired the shot.'

The two Italian prisoners who cooked and served the party that evening, Rosario Schirinzi and Vincenzo Renna, were both interviewed at the hearing. They both recalled hearing eight to ten shots, seeing damaged light fittings and broken glasses and plates afterwards and sweeping away bullet shells on the floor the following morning. Schirinzi was a good friend of Bartoli and had helped carry him on the stretcher to the infirmary on the night that he had been shot.

The hearing continued on Christmas Eve. Captain Waterston was recalled and reminded of his testimony in Justice Simpson's inquest. The transcript was read out where he was asked who fired the shot in the mess that night. At the time he had answered, 'Captain Thomson.'

Captain Waterston was asked if he had spoken to Thomson. He said that they had had several discussions about the shooting and that Thomson indignantly denied that he fired the shots.

Had Captain Thomson been asked to give evidence, he may have found himself in the same position as Waterston and been asked why his account differed from the evidence given at Justice Simpson's inquiry where he said, when questioned about the dinner party, 'A silly bit of foolishness and larking occurred that night and a number of shots were fired by the major and I fired one shot myself.'

Astonishingly, despite Captain Waterston's 'forgetful' evidence, Captain Thomson's previous admission to firing his gun when he gave evidence at Justice Simpson's inquiry and Justice Simpson's comments that he was a witness with no regard for the truth, the court subsequently found Thomson not guilty of the second charge of improperly discharging a firearm in the officers' mess.

At Justice Simpson's recommendation, Major Ruddock didn't perform any inspectional duties. The Adjutant-General recommended that a note be placed on his service record regarding the finding. It was to read: 'As a result of his neglect and incompetence in performing inspectional duties in connection with Prisoner of War Control Hostel V22, Rowville, Major Ruddock is not to be employed at any time, or in any capacity, which would involve similar inspectional duties.'[3]

Major Ruddock wrote a lengthy letter to Southern Command on 30 October 1946. 'With reference to the AHQ instruction that a certain notation be made upon my records, I respectfully desire to point out that although Mr Simpson's finding was in the nature of an adverse report, I was not asked to comment thereon before AHQ came to their conclusion. I, therefore, now request that before the notation is made, the following representations be considered.'

Ruddock explained that he believed that Justice Simpson's finding was based on incomplete evidence. He complained that he had only be asked very few questions and then was 'abruptly dismissed and given no further opportunity to give any more evidence in the inquiry.' He also stated that his inspection was focused on the items in the pro forma inspection document and that he had received no instructions regarding detention huts or cells. He described the Rowville camp as a large hutted camp with many buildings, huts, stores, kitchens, hospitals, messes, recreation rooms, quarters, offices, workshops, ablutions, latrines and drainage systems, all of which Ruddock says he inspected. He states that there were no detention huts in the area during his inspections but he had since heard that there was one some distance away in a part of the Rowville camp not occupied by prisoners. This is despite the fact that it was stated a number of times that the guardroom and detention cells were located by the front gate and main entrance to the camp. Ruddock closed in saying, 'May I state that during my service of four years in the Militia Forces, and thirty-six years in the Permanent Military Forces of Australia, this is the first occasion that I have been accused of any neglect or incompetence in the performance of my military duties.'[4]

Major Ruddock had been relieved of his appointment. For approximately a year after the decision, correspondence continued between the Minister for Army, Cyril Chambers, and the Adjutant-General as to why Major Ruddock's punishment differed from Waterston and Thomson's. The Adjutant-General believed that there had been a misapprehension regarding the meaning of 'relieved of his appointment'. Major Ruddock had ceased all inspection duties in February 1946, and this was deemed sufficient. Dissatisfied with the notation made on his record, Major Ruddock and Southern Command made representations to the Adjutant-General requesting the removal of 'certain derogatory remarks'. The Adjutant-General endorsed that these be expunged from Major Ruddock's record of service.[5]

A minute paper from the Department of Army noted that Justice Simpson's report contained some adverse criticism of the army administration, especially at Rowville and possibly the Murchison Prisoner of War Group. It noted that censorship control on POW correspondence had been removed by this time and prisoners were allowed access to newspapers. Therefore, it was considered undesirable for any criticism to be made public as prisoners 'would no doubt react unfavourably and would possibly cause disturbances or take action which may have unfortunate results.' A handwritten note on the bottom of the minute paper dated 5 September reads, 'Arrangements to this effect have been made with the secretary (Mr Harding). The report is now marked SECRET. 9/9/46.'[6]

CHAPTER 14

After Internment

THERE IS NO NEAT AND HAPPY CONCLUSION TO THIS STORY. Seven official investigations took place: The Military Court of Inquiry into the shooting, a Coroner's Inquest into the death of Bartoli, a formal government inquiry into the alleged mistreatment of prisoners, an independent inquiry into the alleged mistreatment of prisoners and the shooting of Bartoli, two court-martial hearings and a police investigation. Justice Simpson's inquiry was very critical of the administration of the Rowville hostel and found both Thomson and Waterston to be consistently untruthful. There were allegations of prisoners and guards hearing Waterston saying more than once that he wanted to kill an Italian prisoner as well as repeated inconsistencies and discrepancies in both Waterston's and Thomson's evidence. Despite this, the only tangible punishment issued was a reprimand to Captain Waterston for an offence unrelated to the shooting of Rodolfo.

The story that had been circulating around the camp and the local community about the missing iron sheets and speculation that this may have been a motive for the shooting were not investigated. However, Waterston's assault on Quintavalle to force him to make a written statement about the missing iron sheets being a motive for the shooting was one of the charges that Waterston was found guilty of.

We may never know the reason why Waterston fired on Rodolfo that night and whether it was intended as a warning, an attempt to deliberately wound or kill him or just one reckless shot too many.

Sadly, the initial inquiry triggered by the allegations in Mrs Santospirito's letter had been announced just three days before Rodolfo was killed.

The Herald printed the following article on 18 December 1946:

> **All POWs on Way Home Next Month**
> Between now and the end of January, 12,434 Italian and German prisoners of war and 340 internees – all the prisoners of war in Australia – will be repatriated.
>
> Army Headquarters announced today that including the 700 Italians who had sailed from South Australia in the *Moreton Bay* last week, 7837 Italians, 66 Germans and 4294 Japanese prisoners of war had been repatriated.
>
> Prisoners of war will be repatriated as follows – *El Kaniara* to leave Sydney on 23 December with 3323 Italians. *Ormande* to leave Sydney on 24 December with 2037 Italians to pick up 276 in Melbourne and 28 in Fremantle. *Otranto* to leave Melbourne in the Middle of January with 3710 Italians and *Oronies* to leave Melbourne at the end of January with 1270 Italians, 1450 Germans as well as 340 internees of various nationalities.[1]

Many of the Italian prisoners who had been based at Rowville and had appeared at the various inquests began their voyage home to Italy on the *Otranto* and *Oronies* in January 1947.

The Dandenong Journal printed the following article on 9 October 1946:

> **Rowville POW Commander on Another Job**
> The Commanding Officer of the Rowville Italian prisoner of war camp (Capt. Waterston) has been relieved and is doing other work in the Army.

> Conditions in the Rowville prisoner of war camp, when an Italian prisoner of war was shot dead, were investigated recently by Mr Justice Simpson, whose report has not been released.
>
> The report has been handed to the Minister for the Army (Mr Forde), but military officers consider it unlikely to be released, as if unfavourable, it would influence the discipline among Italian prisoners of war, restive because lack of shipping is delaying their repatriation.[2]

Captain Waterston's and Thomson's court-martial hearings were over. Captain Thomson had been relieved of his existing role at the Murchison Prisoner of War Group and was reassigned as Chief Projects Officer for the Murchison Prisoner of War Group. Captain Waterston was posted as Company Officer to B Company. Fortunately for Captain Waterston, Victoria Police notified the Australian military that they did not propose to take any further action against him into the shooting of Rodolfo.

Rodolfo was buried at the Springvale cemetery on 2 April 1946. In 1961, his body was relocated to the Ossario in the Murchison cemetery where 130 people of Italian descent who had passed away in prisoner of war and internment camps all over the country during World War Two have been laid to rest. Each year on Remembrance Day, people gather for Mass at the Mediterranean-style building within the Murchison cemetery to commemorate the Italian internees who lost their lives while in Australia.

The Remembrance Day service at the Ossario at the Murchison Cemetery, November 2018

Rodolfo's plaque at the Ossario in Murchison

One of the former prisoners from Rowville, Phil Faella, returned home on the *Oronies* in January 1947. His family had not been told that he was returning home when he arrived back and an emotional reunion took place when he arrived back after being away for seven years. In 1949, Phil, by then married, wrote to a local Rowville farmer who he had become friends with, George Leeworthy. George sponsored Phil to return to Australia. Phil worked and lived on George's farm in Rowville saving enough money to pay for his wife Maria's voyage out to Australia. Phil, his wife and children lived in Wantirna where Phil worked as a market gardener well into his sixties.[3]

Frank Ponzoni, one of the escapees on the evening of 18 February 1946, married June in September 1947. June's family had helped Frank to escape that night and had provided him with a place to live in hiding. On the eve of their wedding, *The Truth* newspaper had published an article about them: 'Canterbury Girl and POW Escapee in Romance'. Frank and June lived in Italy for a short time. With no work available in Italy, they returned to Australia where they lived in Mont Albert and Frank worked as a commercial artist. After Frank retired in 1976, they moved back to Italy.[4]

The Truth, 20 September 1947[5]

Nora continued to correspond with the Bartoli family: Donatello, Rodolfo's mother, Pia, and his sister, Carla.

> Florence, February 3 1947
>
> Very kind Miss Nora,
> With a very great pleasure we have received your welcome letter where I hear you have send to us 5 packets for the moment we have only received one, that with the wool, but we hope to receive in a short time the others.
>
> I have not enough words to thank you of all what you are doing for us, but I believe that Rodolfo will bless you from heaven. You say to me that my poor Foffo was much surprised when he knew Clara got married, and I too think so because when he departed she was a baby, but six years passed and so she became a woman and she too reached her aim.
>
> We received the pictures were in the letter, you cannot think our surprise in seeing my dear son, you, your father and sisters and brothers that we like very much, you are, sure, all so good, and of all I thank you so much.
>
> I send you two pictures of Rodolfo, when he was a child 8 years old, and one 10 years old, so you will see the like.
>
> I send you best regards from my family and from me many kisses.
>
> Donatello Bartoli

Rodolfo's mother, Pia, wrote to Nora in December 1947.

> 15 December 1947
>
> Dear Nora,
>
> We have received your parcel containing some milk, sugar, coffee and wool. We thank you and not only for these things which are

precious for us but also and chiefly because we see that you remember us.

Christmas is near. In that day we could have been united all together, but an awful destiny has brought my son away. I hope in that holy day you will have a kind thought for him and you will bring a flower on his lovely grave.

If you will have the possibility to come to Italy we should be happy to make your acquaintance and to receive you in our modest home.

I thank you again for everything and I send you all our best wishes for a merry Christmas and a happy new year.

Yours sincerely

Pia Bartoli and family

Eduardo Pizzi had returned to Italy aboard the *Otranto* on 10 January 1947. He sent a typed letter to Nora on 11 March 1947 on his personally monogrammed letterhead.

Rome March 11 1947

Dear Nora,

I'll have to begin this [letter of] mine presenting you my apologies, apologies I owe you for having delayed on writing and for typing this letter.

I'll try to justify the first, saying that only now, after a month since my arrive in Italy, I am getting back to normal; as for my second, my wish to [alleviate] your arduous task of deciphering my horrible handwriting, will be reason enough to excuse me, I hope.

Useless to describe the impression caused by my return to my place in society of human beings, by my newly acquired Freedom, and at last by all I had left so long ago and wanted so badly for many years. I thought that, having been at large in Melbourne, the effect would have been diminished; I was wrong! The wonderful demonstrations of love from my family and of affection from the friends have really shaken me deeply and if to that you add all that a return to normal life implicates for an ex POW, you'll get a pretty good idea about the variety of my feelings.

Dear old Roma is more or less the same, a bit neglected, perhaps. It's queer, but it seems to me as if she were even more beautiful than before.

Now I am working for UNRRA and I have quite a good position already; I have been very lucky, as they are dismissing a lot of personnel and there's a good hope for the future. My intentions are to work and keep on studying at the same time because I can't be a weight for my family today, even if they don't like the idea very much.

In the place I am now working, my position is that of a superintendent and when I see other employees, Checker and labourers working and myself directing them I can't help laughing at the thought of my past experiences as a humble labourer in Australia. (can you imagine how conceited I'll soon become)

Apart [from] the jokes it was just what we needed because my brother is at University, my father is still around and they have spent in the last few years nearly all they had accumulated of late.

But I am being quite rude, talking like that only about me and my happenings, am I not?

How are you? And all the family? I hope everything is fine as it used to be. I often think to the nice evenings we used to spend at your place and I feel a debt of gratitude toward you hoping and wishing to be able one day to repay you, even if in little measure.

Mum would have like to write you but she is still rather upset by my return and she's always got a lot to do, so she told me to express her gratitude for all the comfort you gave me when I needed it so much and to send her kindest regards.

I hope you'll justify my several mistakes, but as I am only a beginner, you'll understand. Having found on the desk of my room a nice modern little typewriter, I set my mind to learn to use it and now I am under training, as I am conceited and want to go fast even at the beginning, you can easily see the terrible result.

And how is the farm going? Have there been any alteration in your life which would be worth mentioning? I hope that in your answer you'll write me all about that and the old friends I used to see, and that I remember with fondness.

I think my writing hasn't been quite correct even in its phrases which are rather disconnected but I have little room to say much and there's always the old reason of my condition of spirit. I am writing to all the friends in Australia, one by one taking my time just for the same reason.

I ask you to remember me to all my old cobbers you'll get the chance to see. Are they safe now or do they feel themselves still in danger?

Now as the sheet doesn't offer much more room I had better bring this letter to a close. Sending all of my thoughts and best greetings and my particular regards to your mother.

Wishing to hear from you is that madman of Eduardo.

Eduardo sent a postcard from Florence, Rodolfo's home city, in 1949. He starts the postcard with Rodolfo's nickname: 'Here from the city of Foffo'.

> Here from the city of Foffo I'm sending you the expression of my friendship. Fond greetings also to all the family and particularly dear Mrs Gearon.

Eduardo
Florence, beautiful & ancient
27 April 1949

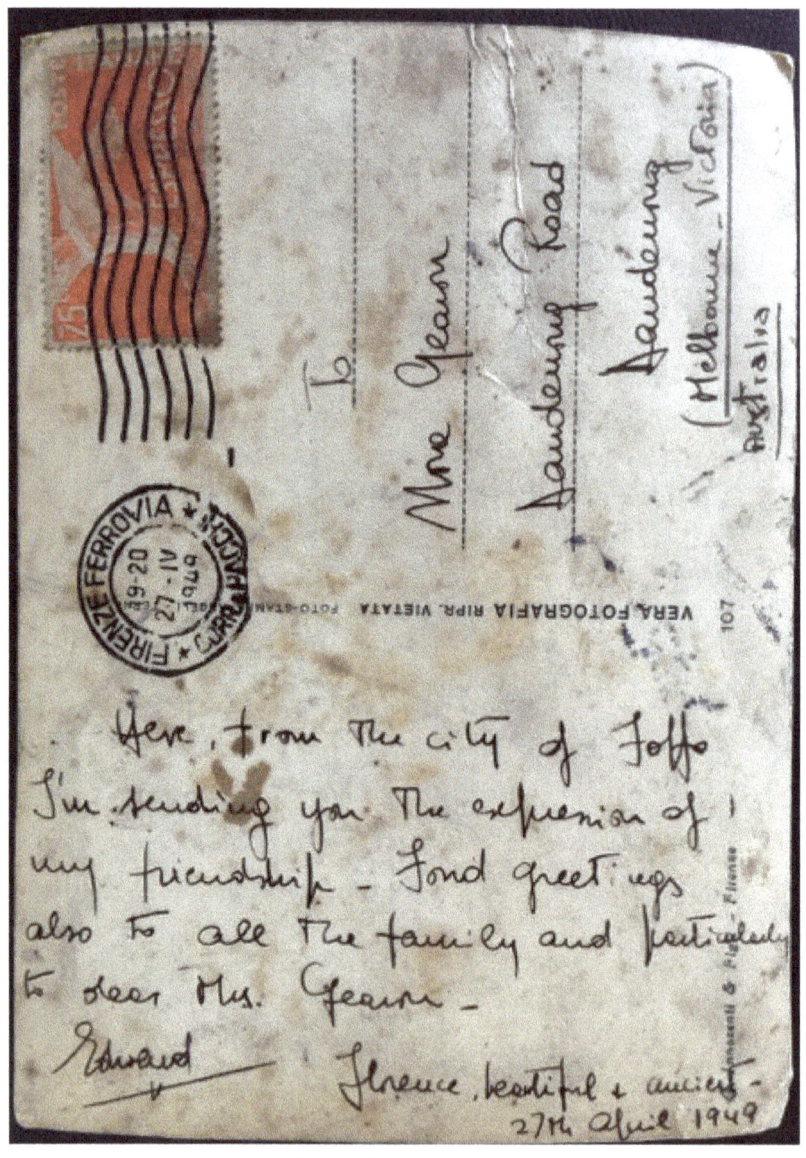

Postcard from Eduardo Pizzi, April 1949

Nora later married Charles O'Ryan and had a family of six children.

With the camp now closed, the land remained unused for many years. For several years in the late 1940s, the roads around the campsite were used for professional motorcycle races and later for horseriding. Most of the camp site is now covered by a large housing estate. Some of the building foundations can still be seen in a section that remains mostly undisturbed near a power transmission station.

Starlight Reserve is a bushland park nestled in the middle of the houses. Within the reserve, a small section of the southern boundary road remains, as well as the concrete foundation block from the latrine featured in the photograph used in both the Coroner's Inquest and Justice Simpson's inquiry.

Detective Adam (foreground) and camp interpreter Sergeant Adamsohn (background) at the scene of the shooting in April 1946; the author at the same place in Starlight Reserve in 2018

Timeline of Events

1940

10 December 1940 – Rodolfo Bartoli captured in Libya

1941

15 October 1941 – Rodolfo Bartoli arrives in Australia

1943

30 March 1943 – John Waterston promoted to Captain

1944

December 1944 – Rowville Prisoner of War camp commences with 100 prisoners
December 1944 – Rodolfo arrives in Rowville
January 1944 – Prisoner numbers at Rowville increase to 150

1945

February 1945 – Captain Waterston becomes Camp Commandant at Rowville
April 1945 – Captain Waterston discharges firearm in mess hut
8 May 1945 – VE (Victory in Europe) Day, the end of the war in Europe
22 May 1945 – Harley and Haggis visit
5 June 1945 – Role of Rowville camp changed to a staging camp
12 June 1945 – Camp leader Parisi writes official letter of complaint, letter never delivered
26 July 1945 – Prisoner numbers at Rowville increase to 200
August 1945 – Prisoner numbers at Rowville increase to 250

15 August 1945 – VP (Victory in the Pacific) Day, the end of the war in the Pacific
December 1945 – Captain Waterston fires his pistol into the roof in the cells

1946
18 February 1946 – Eight prisoners escape
1 March 1946 – Letter of complaint sent from Mrs Santospirito to Mr Calwell
27 March 1946 – Major Archer appointed to head inquiry into alleged mistreatment of prisoners
30 March 1946 – Captain Waterston assaults Viviani and Guglielmetti and places them in detention without charge
30 March 1946 – Captain Waterston shoots and kills Rodolfo Bartoli
5 April 1946 – Military Court of Inquiry held at Rowville; Waterston found to be justified in his actions
5 April 1946 – Dinner party at Rowville Camp, Captain Thomson, Major Archer and Captain Waterston present; shots are fired by them at the lights and into the roof
8 April 1946 – Major Archer undertakes his inquiry into allegations of mistreatment of prisoners
8 April 1946 – Justice Simpson's inquiry announced
9 April 1946 – Homicide squad detectives visit the camp with representatives from the Swiss Consul to collect evidence in preparation for the Coroner's Inquest
16 April 1946 – Major Archer's inquiry is complete; his report finds the allegations to be unsubstantiated
14 May 1946 – Captain Waterston assaults Enrico Quintavalle
15 May 1946 – Coroner's Inquest into the death of Rodolfo Bartoli
21 June 1946 – Justice Simpson's inquiry into allegations of mistreatment of prisoners, the administration of the camp and the death of Rodolfo Bartoli commences
27 August 1946 – Justice Simpson's report released
16 December 1946 – Captain Waterston's court-martial hearing commences

23 December 1946 – Captain Thomson's court-martial hearing commences

1947
January 1947 – Victorian-based Italian prisoners of war begin their journey home

Witnesses at Military Court of Inquiry

Giuseppe Galli – Italian 2nd Lieutenant, camp doctor
Leslie Keith Holtham – Australian Sergeant
Hugh McDougall – Australian Warrant Officer
William Ian Purbrick – Australian Lieutenant
Rosario Schirinzi – Italian infantry soldier
Michele Scuma – Italian Staff Sergeant, camp leader
Herbert James Thomson – Australian Company Commander
Enrico Veronelli – Italian Private
John Westlake Wales – doctor, Heidelberg Hospital
John Walker Waterston – Australian Captain

Witnesses Called at the Coroner's Inquest

Detective John Adam – Homicide detective
Raffaele Ciuffi – Italian POW
Amilcare Dini – Italian POW
Joseph Galli – Italian camp doctor
Edmond James Gearon – Farmer
Giacomo Grassi – Italian POW
Leslie Keith Holtham – Australian Sergeant
Adamo Marsi – Italian POW
Leo Francis McCarthy – Australian Corporal
Hugh McDougall– Australian Warrant Officer
Crawford Henry Mollison – Australian surgeon
Pasquale Papa – Italian POW
Francisco Pellicano – Italian POW
Carmelo Perugini – Italian POW
Charles Herbert Petty – Homicide detective
William Ian Purbrick – Australian Army
Enrico Quintavalle – Italian POW
Joseph Raimondi – Italian POW, padre
Rosario Schirinzi – Italian POW
Michele Scuma – Italian camp leader
Charles Anthony Taylor – medical chemist
Herbert James Thomson – Australian Captain
Corinto Tosi – Italian POW
Enrico Veronelli – Italian POW
John Westlake Wales – Medical Corps, Heidelberg Hospital
John Walker Waterston – Australian Captain

Witnesses Called at Justice Simpson's Inquiry

Frederick John Adam – Homicide detective, Victoria Police
Dini Amilcare – Italian Corporal Major
Vincenzo Andreucci – Italian Private
Austin Purchase Appelby – Australian Adjutant, Murchison
WIlliam Charles Honnis Baggs – Victoria Police
William Ephraim Banks – Constable, Victoria Police Wireless Patrol
Andrea Battaglia – Italian Navy, waiter on ship
Rodolfo Beltino – Italian Seaman
Zaccaria Bosa – resident, Springvale
Keith Bridgland – Australian driver
Kenneth John Mackenzie Bullock – Australian driver
Silvio Buriassi – Italian Private
Amedeo Cacciagrano – Italian Private
Alfonso Cagnese – Italian Black Shirt
Eugenio Calliste – Italian Private
Domenico Capriotti – Italian Private
Torquinio Catena – Italian Private
Raffaele Ciuffa – Italian Private
Michael Francis Costello – Australian Sergeant, interpreter
Generoso Cresta – Italian Sergeant Major
Gian Battista Di Franco – Italian prisoner, rank unknown
Giovanni Dutto – Italian Finance/Customs Guard
Ottavio Faccini – Italian Sergeant
Emidio Ferrone – Italian Infantryman
John Joseph Finn – farmer, Rowville
Lieutenant Colonel J W Flannagan – Australian Lieutenant Colonel

Witnesses Called at Justice Simpson's Inquiry

Guerrino Fornisaro – Italian Private
Angelo Franchitto – Italian Private
Saverio Fulginiti – Italian Private
Togo Funicella – Italian Corporal Major
Ottavio Furia – Italian Private
Giuseppe Galli – Italian 2nd Lieutenant, camp doctor
Vincenzo Gigliotti – Italian Corporal Major
Giaccono Grassa – Italian Corporal Major
Attilio Guglielmetti – Italian Seaman
Henry Baynton Gullett – farmer, politician
Leslie Thomas Harley – Victoria Police
Gerald Paul Healy – legal officer
James Guy Heynemann – Australian Sergeant, interpreter
Henry Robert Hodge – Constable, Wireless Patrol
Leslie Keith Holtham – Australian Military, interpreter
Francesco Lo Crasto – Italian Merchant Seaman
James Lloyd Logan – Australian Corporal
Adolfo Maffei – Italian Private
Giuseppe Marchiafava – Italian Private
Domenico Marinuzzi – Italian Corporal
Adamo Marsi – Italian Private
Sydney Arthur Bruce Mathers – Australian Staff Sergeant
Ottavio Mazzola – Italian Private
David Thomas McAvoy – Constable, Wireless Patrol
Lee Francis McCarthy – Australian Corporal
George William McDonald – Australian driver
Hugh McDougall – Australian Warrant Officer
Frederick Norman McKinnon – Australian Corporal
Phillip Clarence McLaren – Australian Lieutenant
William Henry McMennemin – Senior Detective, Victoria Police
Vittorio Micillo – Italian Navy
Giuseppe Minichiello – Italian Private
Ernesto Musiari – Italian Lieutenant
Mattia Natale – Italian Private

Natalio Nesti – Italian Corporal Major
Giuseppe Nestico – Italian Private
Francesco Nicosia – Italian Merchant Marine
Giovanni Nuzzarello – Italian Private
Pasquale Paka – Italian Private
Umberto Paolesse – Italian Private
Romano Papini – Italian Infantry Sergeant
Giuseppe Parisi – Italian Sergeant
Francesco Pellicano – Italian Navy
Carmine Perugini – Italian Private
Charles Herbert Petty – homicide detective, Victoria Police
Rinaldo Pisacane – Italian Private
Eduardo Ezio Pizzi – Italian Private
Aldo Poggi – Italian Private
Eric James Poole – Australian Sergeant
Gaetano Prochilo – Italian Private
William Ian Purbrick – Australian Lieutenant
Enrico Quintavalle – Italian Sailor
Josef Raimondi – Italian Lieutenant, padre
Vincenzo Renna – Italian Private
Karl Ritter – Secretary to Delegate of the protecting power for the prisoners of war
Major William Cyril Gentry Ruddock – Australian Major
Donald Alexander Sandy – Australian Major
Gaetano Scalici – Italian Black Shirt
Mario Scatena – Italian Sergeant
Rosario Schirinzi – Italian infantry soldier
Michele Scuma – Italian Staff Sergeant, camp leader
Robert Adrian Seymour – Australian Warrant Officer
Colin Smith – Australian driver
Antonio Soldano – Italian Private
Salvatore Spedicato – Italian Corporal Major
Enrico Spurio – Italian Corporal
Keith Stone – Australian driver

Witnesses Called at Justice Simpson's Inquiry

Michele Stoppello – Italian Private
Luke Strickland – Australian Captain
Alcide Stucchi – Italian Corporal
Herbert James Thomson – Australian Company Commander
Corinto Tosi – Italian Private
Ricardo Trucco – Italian Medical Officer
Salvatore Valentino – Italian Private
Enrico Veronelli – Italian Private
Eugenio Visione – Italian Merchant Navy
Silvano Viviani – Italian Private
John Westlake Wales – doctor, Heidelberg Hospital
John Walker Waterston – Australian Captain
Romeo Zuzzaro – Italian Black Shirt

Witnesses Called at Captain Waterston's Court Martial

William Charles Honiss Baggs – Australian Army
Amedeo Cacciagrano – Italian POW
Giovanni Dutto – Italian POW
Attilio Guglielmetti – Italian POW
Leslie Keith Holtham – Australian interpreter
Giuseppe Marchiafava – Italian POW
Sydney Arthur Bruce Mathers – Australian Pay corps
Hugh McDougall – Australian Sergeant Major
Natalino Nesti – Italian POW
Giuseppe Parisi – Italian POW
Eduardo Ezio Pizzi – Italian POW
William Ian Purbrick – Australian Lieutenant
Enrico Quintavalle – Italian POW
Herbert James Thomson – Australian Captain
Silvano Viviani – Italian POW
John Walker Waterston – Australian Captain

Witnesses Called at Captain Thomson's Court Martial

Vincenzo Renna – Italian Private
Rosario Schirinzi – Italian infantry soldier
Colonel Walter Noel Tinsley – Commanding Officer, Murchison
Captain John Walker Waterston – Australian Captain

Maps

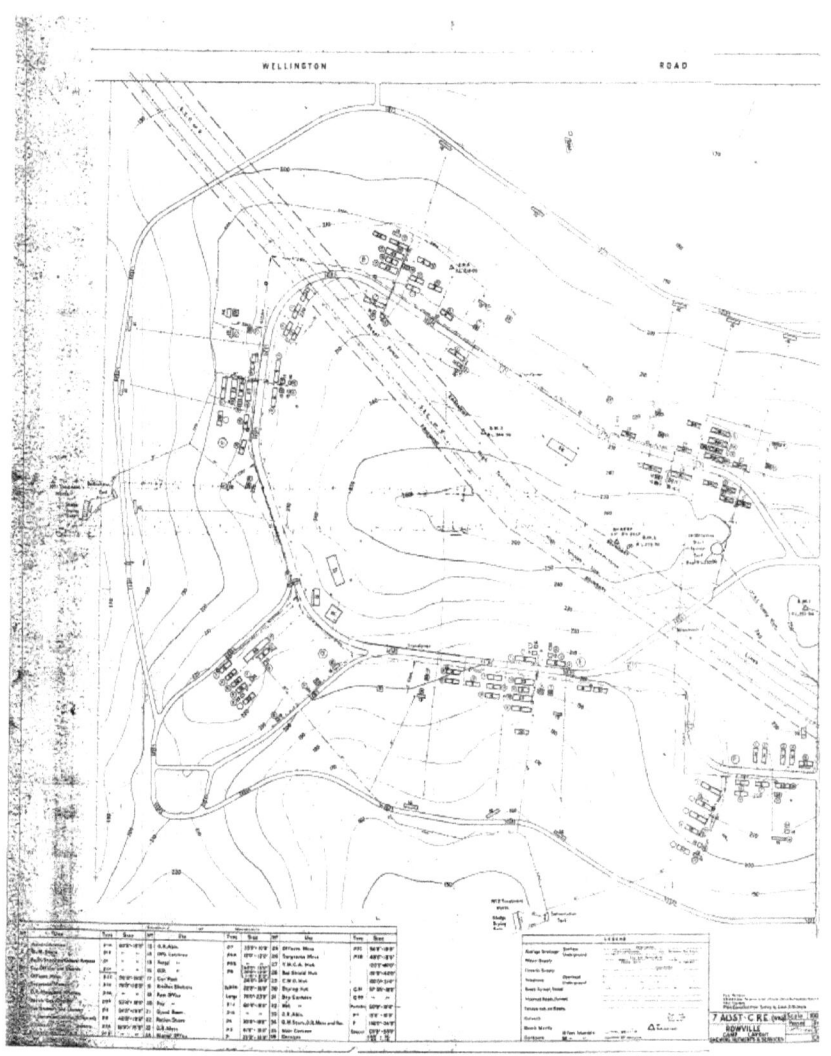

Rowville Military Camp, 1942. Used by the Australian Army and US Marines prior to being an Italian Prisoner of War camp[1]

Endnotes

Chapter 1

1. Fitzgerald, Alan, 1981, *The Italian Farming Soldiers: Prisoners of War in Australia 1941–1947,* Melbourne University Press, Melbourne

2. Fitzgerald, Alan, 1981, *The Italian Farming Soldiers: Prisoners of War in Australia 1941–1947,* Melbourne University Press, Melbourne

3. In reference by the Minister of State for the Army in relation to the administration of Rowville Prisoner of War Control Hostel, and the circumstances resulting in the death of an Italian prisoner of war No. 48833 R. Bartoli. NAA: MP742/1, 255-6-774 Part 1

4. Coulson, Helen, 1959, *Story of the Dandenongs,* FW Cheshire Publishing, Melbourne

5. *Stocktaking Sheet, Rations, PWCC Rowville.* NAA: MP742/1, 255-6-774 Part 1

6. *Rosehill[sic] (Dandenong) Camp, these huts at present empty,* http://search.slv.vic.gov.au/MAIN:Everything:SLV_VOYAGER1707251, Argus Newspaper Collection of Photographs, State Library of Victoria

7. Power, Bryan, 2005, 'Brian Seymour Remembers the Friendly POWs at Rowville', *Rowville & Lysterfield Stories, Rowville–Lysterfield Community News*

Chapter 2

1. O'Ryan, Nora & Riddell, Carmel, interview by Darren Arnott, 14 April 2019
2. *Statement taken from Captain Waterston by Detective PH Petty, 9/4/463.* Exhibit No 28. NAA: MP742/1, 255-6-774 Part 2
3. *Prisoners of War Camp Order No. 13.* Exhibit No 2. NAA: MP742/1, 255-6-774 Part 2

Chapter 3

1. Santospirito, Lena to Hon. Arthur Calwell, 1 March 1946. NAA: MP742/1, 255-6-774 Part 1
2. 'Louisa Angelina (Lena) Santospirito', http://www.coasit.com.au/ihs/sant/SANP001.htm#1, accessed 6 September 2018
3. Sinclair, Frank to Adjutant-General, Capt. Waterston POW Camp, Springvale, 21 March 1946. NAA: MP742/1, 255-6-774 Part 1
4. Adjutant-General to Southern Command, PWC Hostel – V22 Rowville, 27 March 1946. NAA: MP742/1, 255-6-774 Part 1
5. Southern Command Headquarters to Major HJ Archer, Appointment as Investigating Officer into Allegation of Ill-treatment of PW at PWCH V.22 Rowville. NAA: MP742/1, 255-6-774 Part 1

Chapter 4

1. '5 of 14 escapees caught', *The Herald* (Melbourne, Vic.: 1861–1954), 18 February 1946, p. 3, viewed 7 March 2018, http://nla.gov.au/nla.news-article245949480
2. *Rough Diary PWC V.22 Rowville.* Exhibit 35. NAA: MP742/1, 255-6-774 Part 1

Endnotes

3. Power, Bryan, 2005, 'Betty Jenkins (nee Drummond) Remembers Growing up at Stamford Park', *Rowville & Lysterfield Stories*, *Rowville–Lysterfield Community News*

4. Inquiry into the administration and matters surrounding the administration of the prisoner of war hostel, Rowville Victoria. Eduardo Pizzi 21 June 1946. NAA: MP742/1, 255-6-774 Part 1

5. O'Ryan, Nora & Riddell, Carmel, interview by Darren Arnott, 14 April 2019

6. 'Arrested in his new brown suit', *The Herald* (Melbourne, Vic.: 1861–1954), 16 December 1946, p. 5, http://nla.gov.au/nla.news-article245384161

7. Power, Bryan, 2006, *Rowville & Lysterfield Stories*

8. *Victoria Police Gazette*, 25 January 1946, p. 2

9. Power, Bryan, 2006, 'Scandal as Melbourne Girl Weds Escapee from Rowville POW Camp', *Rowville & Lysterfield Stories*, *Rowville–Lysterfield Community News*, accessed 6 January 2018, http://pandora.nla.gov.au/pan/49499/20070616-0000/www.rlcnews.org.au/stories/army_camp_pow_camp/scandal_as_melbourne_girl_weds_escapee_from_rowville_pow_camp.html

10. *Victoria Police Gazette*, March 1946, p. 98

11. *Copy of report sent in by wireless car to Russell St.* Exhibit 26. NAA: MP742/1, 255-6-774 Part 2

12. Inquisition held at City Morgue – Melbourne – On the Body of Rodolfo Bartoli 15 May 1946. PROV, VPRS 24 P0 1547

13. Inquiry into the administration and matters surrounding the administration of the prisoner of war hostel, Rowville Victoria. DT McAvoy and HR Hodge 13 August 1946. NAA: MP742/1, 255-6-774 Part 1

14. *Rough Diary PWC V.22 Rowville.* Exhibit 35. NAA: MP742/1, 255-6-774 Part 2

15. 'Army explains POW shooting case', *The Herald* (Melbourne, Vic.: 1861–1954), 1 April 1946, p. 7, http://nla.gov.au/nla.news-article245396673
16. *Victoria Police Gazette*, 4 April 1946, p. 1
17. Sinclair, Frank to Forde, Francis, POW Camp – Rowville, 1 April 1946. NAA: MP742/1, 255-6-774 Part 1
18. Sinclair, Frank to Adjutant-General, POW Camp – Rowville, 1 April 1946. NAA: MP385/7, 53/101/420
19. Forde, Francis to Sinclair Frank, 2 April 1946. NAA: MP742/1, 255-6-774 Part 1
20. *The Truth*, 4 April 1946, p. 1, photograph of original article from June Ponzoni's collection
21. O'Ryan, Nora & Riddell, Carmel, interview by Darren Arnott, 14 April 2019
22. Inquiry into the administration and matters surrounding the administration of the prisoner of war hostel, Rowville Victoria. Romano Papina 6 August 1946. NAA: MP742/1, 255-6-774 Part 1

Chapter 5

1. *Plan of Camp Boundaries.* Exhibit 23. NAA: MP742/1, 255-6-774 Part 2
2. Proceedings of Court of Inquiry assembled at Rowville, 5 April 1946. NAA: MP385/7
3. Inquiry into the administration and matters surrounding the administration of the prisoner of war hostel, Rowville Victoria. Captain HJ Thomson 13 August 1946. NAA: MP742/1, 255-6-774 Part 1
4. Forde, Francis to Secretary, Death by Shooting – PWI 48833, Bartoli, Rodolfo, 3 May 1946. NAA: MP742/1, 255-6-774 Part 1

13. Inquiry into the administration and matters surrounding the administration of the prisoner of war hostel, Rowville Victoria. Transcript of evidence from Aldo Poggi 6 August 1946. NAA: MP742/1, 255-6-774 Part 1

14. Inquisition held at City Morgue – Melbourne – On the Body of Rodolfo Bartoli 15 May 1946. *Coroner's Report.* PROV, VPRS 24 P0 1547

15. Inquiry into the administration and matters surrounding the administration of the prisoner of war hostel, Rowville Victoria. Hugh McDougall 9 August 1946. NAA: MP742/1, 255-6-774 Part 1

16. Inquisition held at City Morgue – Melbourne – On the Body of Rodolfo Bartoli 15 May 1946. *Coroner's Report.* Captain Waterston. PROV, VPRS 24 P0 1547

17. *The Truth*, 25 May 1946, p. 8, photograph of original article from June Ponzoni's collection

18. Scuma, Michele to Swiss Consulate and the International Red Cross, 3 April 1946. NAA: MP385/7

19. Inquiry into the administration and matters surrounding the administration of the prisoner of war hostel, Rowville Victoria. Enrico Quintavalle's statement. Exhibit 17. NAA: MP742/1, 255-6-774 Part 2

Chapter 9

1. Forde FM Minister for Army, Letter appointing Justice Simpson outlining the allegations for terms of reference, 8 April 1946. NAA: MP742/1, 255-6-774 Part 1

2. Inquiry into the administration and matters surrounding the administration of the prisoner of war hostel, Rowville Victoria. Transcript of evidence from Gerald Healy 25 May 1946. NAA: MP742/1, 255-6-774 Part 1

3. WATERSTON John Walker : Service Number – VX5238 : Date of birth – 18 Feb 1912 : Place of birth – ST KILDA VIC : Place of enlistment – BENDIGO VIC : Next of Kin – WATERSTON John. NAA: B883, VX5238

4. Tait, AWM 058227

5. Inquiry into the administration and matters surrounding the administration of the prisoner of war hostel, Rowville Victoria. Captain Waterston 14 August 1946. NAA: MP742/1, 255-6-774 Part 1

6. Power, Bryan, 2005, 'Phil Faella Remembers his time as a POW at Rowville', *Rowville–Lysterfield Community News*

7. Inquiry into the administration and matters surrounding the administration of the prisoner of war hostel, Rowville Victoria. Attilio Guglielmetti 29 May 1946 and Silvano Viviani 10 July 1946. NAA: MP742/1, 255-6-774 Part 1

8. Inquiry into the administration and matters surrounding the administration of the prisoner of war hostel, Rowville Victoria. Leslie Harley 21 June 1946 and Captain Waterston 15 August 1946. NAA: MP742/1, 255-6-774 Part 1

9. *The Herald* (Melbourne, Vic.: 1861–1954), 20 June 1946, p. 22, accessed 7 September 2018, http://nla.gov.au/nla.news-page26692264

10. 'Airman gets £200 for broken jaw', *The Daily Telegraph* (Sydney, NSW: 1931–1954), 27 September 1946, p. 5, accessed 2 Jun 2019, http://nla.gov.au/nla.news-article248577943

11. Documentation supplied from Victoria Police Museum via email 7 September 2018

12. Inquiry into the administration and matters surrounding the administration of the prisoner of war hostel, Rowville Victoria. Giuseppe Marchiafava & Eduardo Pizzi 21 June 1946. NAA: MP742/1, 255-6-774 Part 1

13. Inquiry into the administration and matters surrounding the administration of the prisoner of war hostel, Rowville Victoria. Amedeo Cacciagrano & Natalino Nesti 11 July 1946. NAA: MP742/1, 255-6-774 Part 1

14. Inquiry into the administration and matters surrounding the administration of the prisoner of war hostel, Rowville Victoria. Giuseppe Umberto Paolesse 30 May 1946. NAA: MP742/1, 255-6-774 Part 1

15. Inquiry into the administration and matters surrounding the administration of the prisoner of war hostel, Rowville Victoria. Lee McCarthy 12 August 1946. NAA: MP742/1, 255-6-774 Part 1

16. Inquiry into the administration and matters surrounding the administration of the prisoner of war hostel, Rowville Victoria. Captain Waterston 16 August 1946. NAA: MP742/1, 255-6-774 Part 1

17. *Captain Waterston's Statement taken immediately after the shooting – Australian Military Forces – Vic. L of C Area.* Inquiry into the administration and matters surrounding the administration of the prisoner of war hostel, Rowville Victoria. NAA: MP742/1, 255-6-774 Part 1

18. *Rough plan drawn by His Honour.* Exhibit 22. NAA: MP742/1, 255-6-774 Part 1

Chapter 10

1. Power, Bryan, 2005, 'Shops in Rowville', *Rowville & Lysterfield Stories, Rowville–Lysterfield Community News*

2. 'Twice-heard court case', *The Dandenong Journal* (Vic.: 1927–1954), 17 July 1946, p. 1, accessed 9 Aug 2018, http://nla.gov.au/nla.news-article214794546

3. Inquiry into the administration and matters surrounding the administration of the prisoner of war hostel, Rowville Victoria. John Finn 18 July 1946. NAA: MP742/1, 255-6-774 Part 1

4. Inquiry into the administration and matters surrounding the administration of the prisoner of war hostel, Rowville Victoria. Major Donald Sandy 14 August 1946. NAA: MP742/1, 255-6-774 Part 1

5. *Reports made by Major Ruddock on Rowville Administration. Prisoners of War – Rural Employment Inspection Report No 120. 7 February 1946.* Exhibit 24. NAA: MP742/1, 255-6-774 Part 1

6. Inquiry into the administration and matters surrounding the administration of the prisoner of war hostel, Rowville Victoria. Detective William McMennemin 18 July 1946. NAA: MP742/1, 255-6-774 Part 1

7. [WATERSTON John Walker (Captain): Service Number – VX5238: Unit – Murchison Prisoner of War Group, Australian Military Forces: Date of Court Martial – 16 December 1946] NAA: A471, 79821

8. O'Ryan, Nora & Riddell, Carmel, interview by Darren Arnott, 14 April 2019

Chapter 11

1. Scuma, Michele to Swiss Consulate and the International Red Cross. 3 April 1946. NAA: MP385/7

2. Inquiry into the administration and matters surrounding the administration of the prisoner of war hostel, Rowville Victoria. Captain Herbert Thomson 13 August 1946. NAA: MP742/1, 255-6-774 Part 1

3. Inquiry into the administration and matters surrounding the administration of the prisoner of war hostel, Rowville Victoria.

Major William Ruddock 12 August 1946. NAA: MP742/1, 255-6-774 Part 1

Chapter 12

1. *Australian Military Forces Minute Paper 5 September 1946 – Rowville Enquiry – Administration of Prisoners of War.* Inquiry into the administration and matters surrounding the administration of the prisoner of war hostel, Rowville Victoria. NAA: MP742/1, 255-6-774 Part 1

2. *In the matter of a reference by the Minister of State for the Army in relation to the administration of Rowville Prisoner of War Control Hostel, and the circumstances resulting in the death of an Italian prisoner of war, No. 48833 R. Bartoli. Justice Simpson's Final Report 27 August 1946.* Inquiry into the administration and matters surrounding the administration of the prisoner of war hostel, Rowville Victoria. NAA: MP742/1, 255-6-774 Part 1

Chapter 13

1. [WATERSTON John Walker (Captain) : Service Number – VX5238 : Unit – Murchison Prisoner of War Group, Australian Military Forces : Date of Court Martial – 16 December 1946] NAA: A471, 79821

2. [THOMSON Herbert James (Captain) : Service Number – VX8100 : Unit – Murchison Prisoner War Group, Australian Military Forces : Date of Court Martial – 23 December 1946] NAA: A471, 79310

3. *Adjutant General to Secretary, Department of Army. Prisoner of War Hostel 28 October 1946.* Inquiry into the administration and matters surrounding the administration of the prisoner of war hostel, Rowville Victoria. NAA: MP742/1, 255-6-774 Part 1

4. *Major William Ruddock to Southern Command. Prisoner of Ware Control Hostel V-22 Rowville Commission of Inquiry. Ref AHQ*

SM.1314 of 30 Oct 46. Inquiry into the administration and matters surrounding the administration of the prisoner of war hostel, Rowville Victoria. NAA: MP742/1, 255-6-774 Part 1

5. *Adjutant-General to Secretary, Department of the Army. Rowville Prisoner of War Camp 2 February 1947.* Inquiry into the administration and matters surrounding the administration of the prisoner of war hostel, Rowville Victoria. NAA: MP742/1, 255-6-774 Part 1

6. *Australian Military Forces Minute Paper 5 September 1946 – Rowville Enquiry – Administration of Prisoners of War.* Inquiry into the administration and matters surrounding the administration of the prisoner of war hostel, Rowville Victoria. NAA: MP742/1, 255-6-774 Part 1

Chapter 14

1. 'All POWs on way home next month', *The Herald* (Melbourne, Vic.: 1861–1954), 18 December 1946, p. 9, accessed 3 March 2018, http://nla.gov.au/nla.news-article245386533

2. 'Rowville POW commander on another job', The Dandenong Journal (Vic.: 1927–1954), 9 October 1946, p. 12, accessed 3 March 2018, http://nla.gov.au/nla.news-article214795890

3. Power, Bryan, 2005, 'Phil Faella remembers his time as a POW at Rowville', *Rowville–Lysterfield Community News*

4. Power, Bryan, 2006, 'Scandal as Melbourne girl weds escapee from Rowville POW camp', *Rowville & Lysterfield Stories*, accessed 6 January 2018, http://pandora.nla.gov.au/pan/49499/20070616-0000/www.rlcnews.org.au/stories/army_camp_pow_camp/scandal_as_melbourne_girl_weds_escapee_from_rowville_pow_camp.html

5. *The Truth*, 20 September 1947, photograph of original article from June Ponzoni's collection

Endnotes

Maps

1. *Plan of Area of Rowville Camp.* Exhibit 1. NAA: MP742/1, 255-6-774 Part 2

Acknowledgements

Thank you to those how have helped along the way and have contributed to this book. Thank you to my family Nadia, Emily and Sam for being supportive of my many hours in front of the keyboard and occasionally accompanying me on my archive visits. To Hazel Edwards and the writing group at the Public Record Office Victoria for help with workshopping the chapters as the story came together. Thank you to Bryan Power for recommendations on structure and for providing photographs and additional stories along the way. To those who read my early drafts, Nadia Arnott, Billie and Ray Wyckelsma, Pauline McDonald and my editor Susan Pierotti. Thank you to Greg and Angelina Arena for taking on the challenge of translating Rodolfo's letters and Rodolfo's family's letters from Italian to English.

Finally, a huge thank you to the members of the Gearon family, Rosemary Hawke, Robert Gearon and Gabrielle O'Ryan. A special thank you to Nora O'Ryan and Carmel Riddell for sharing their personal stories, memories, letters and photographs.

About the Author

Darren Arnott is a Melbourne based IT Security Consultant. Outside of work, he was a former editor for The Rowville-Lysterfield Community News. He enjoys history research and writing and has undertaken studies in history and archaeology.

www.darrenarnott.com

www.ingramcontent.com/pod-product-compliance
Lightning Source LLC
Chambersburg PA
CBHW040256170426
43192CB00020B/2826